OUTDOOR ACTION GAMES FOR ELEMENTARY CHILDREN

Active Games & Academic Activities for Fun & Fitness

DAVID R. FOSTER ♦ JAMES L. OVERHOLT

PARKER PUBLISHING COMPANY
West Nyack, New York 10995

This book is dedicated to my students,
for they are the ones that show me how to play.

Mr. Foster

10 9 8 7 6 5 4 3 2 1

Library of Congress Cataloging-in-Publication Data

Foster, David R.
  Outdoor action games for elementary children : active games and
academic activities for fun and fitness / David R. Foster, James L.
Overholt ; illustrations by Ron Schultz.
        p.   cm.
   ISBN 0-13-009895-7
   1. Physical education for children. 2. Outdoor recreation for
children. 3. Games. I. Overholt, James L.   II. Schultz, Ron.
III. Title.
GV443.F66   1994
372.86—dc20
                                                           93–34562
                                                           CIP

ISBN 0-13-009895-7

Parker Publishing Company
Career & Personal Development
West Nyack, NY 10995

Simon & Schuster, A Paramount Communications Company

Printed in the United States of America

ABOUT THIS RESOURCE

In these times, when so many young people are not active on their own, schools must take the lead in teaching students that physical fitness and exercise can be fun, healthy, and can improve their lives both now and in the future. Our purpose is to provide elementary school teachers, physical education instructors, recreation directors and others with a wide selection of playground and academically-based physical education activities. This book is not meant to replace an existing curriculum; rather it is intended as a helpful and enjoyable supplement of fun and challenging physical education games and activities.

Emphasis on school-based physical education fades and resurfaces periodically. Varied trends take shape and "new" emphases continually modify or replace existing methods. Viewpoints of most educators range from the idea that physical education is the most important of all subjects, to the notion that it should be eliminated from the curriculum altogether. In any case, it is clear that children like to play and that they enjoy participating in good physical education programs. In fact, research clearly shows that daily participation by students in physical activities allows for the

- development of health and fitness,
- improvement of skills necessary for mental and physical development,
- release of mental tension accumulated during a strenuous school day,
- recreation necessary for students to remain academically productive throughout each school day, and
- development of interests that contribute to a healthier and happier adult life.

Research further reveals a positive correlation between physical activity and academic success. Students who are given the chance to engage in periodic physical activity during the school day work more efficiently and accomplish more than students denied the opportunity for stimulating exercise.

Students and teachers differ in their likes and dislikes. Therefore, this book provides for a wide range of activities that include varied styles for teaching and participating in physical education. While some of the games can be competitive, others promote cooperation and self-testing. Many of the activities are designed to improve one skill in isolation, while others are more complex and involve several skills. A number of the games are designed specifically to promote teamwork and foster sportsmanship. Some activities require strenuous physical activity or focus on fundamental skills, while others simply promote laughter and smiles. One section of the book provides ideas that allow teachers to incorporate academic material from a variety of subject areas into the physical education program. Regardless of a person's style and philosophy of physical education, many challenging and enjoyable activities are readily available in this resource.

We recommend utilizing activities from each section. In doing so, you will promote cooperation, skill development, sportsmanship, and a sense of enjoyment for health and physical fitness. The activities in this book will help make your school curriculum productive and satisfying for you as an educator, as well as fun and rewarding for your students.

David R. Foster
James L. Overholt

ABOUT THE AUTHORS

David R. Foster, M.Ed. (California State University, Chico) currently teaches sixth grade at Parkview Elementary School in Chico, California. He also teaches physical education activity courses for California State University, and provides school district in-service workshops. He served previously as a fifth and sixth grade teacher at Fairview Elementary School in Orland, California and at Terrace Middle School, Lakeport, California, and worked as a student aide in grades 4 through 6. Mr. Foster also coached boys' and girls' volleyball, basketball, and baseball, and did his Master's thesis on the subject of indoor physical education/recess activities in elementary school classrooms.

James L. Overholt, Ed.D. (University of Wyoming, Laramie) has over 30 years of experience as a public school educator. He began his career teaching in the public schools of LeSueur and Albert Lea, Minnesota, then served as a mathematics teacher/coordinator and instructor in Elementary and Junior High School Education at the University School, University of Wyoming. Presently Dr. Overholt is Professor of Education at California State University, Chico, where he specializes in the areas of student teaching, in-service education, and mathematics education.

Foster and Overholt coauthored *Indoor Action Games for Elementary Children,* published by Parker Publishing Company.

SUGGESTIONS FOR USING *OUTDOOR ACTION GAMES*

The activities within this resource have been categorized by grade level and purpose(s) for convenience. However, we realize that you, the teacher, are ultimately the most qualified person to determine appropriate activities for your particular students. Thus, since many of the activities can be successfully implemented for nearly any age or grade level, please make use of each activity in as many ways as possible.

We also urge users of this resource to take advantage of the suggested variations included for each activity. You will find that many variations foster enthusiasm and continued interest for or by the participants.

As fellow teachers we realize the importance of offering activities that require minimal preparation and equipment. These factors have been given careful consideration throughout the book. A number of the activities require basic equipment commonly found on school campuses, and a few call for additional items that can be gathered, made, received as donations, or purchased. Thus, by checking to see that the items listed in the appendix are available, you will be able to utilize all of the activities in this book effectively for years to come, and will wisely have spent a minimal amount of time, money, and preparation.

We would also like to offer a safety precaution. The games herein are quite safe; however, it is always wise to establish and enforce regulations for safe play. Therefore, we recommend that the involved teacher or leader adhere to guidelines such as the ones that follow:

- Promote cooperation among participants.
- State or review safety rules prior to beginning any activity.
- Have players complete appropriate warm-ups before engaging in strenuous activities.
- Note a signal that will "freeze" everyone if a dangerous situation should occur (for example, blowing a whistle).
- Closely monitor and enforce all guidelines at all times.

In conclusion, we hope that you will find this resource to be a meaningful supplement to your curriculum. We urge you to experiment with several activities from each section appropriate to your physical education program and style of teaching. Finally, our desire is that you and your students engage in stimulating exercises while having a great deal of fun.

TABLE OF CONTENTS

About This Resource .... *iii*

About the Authors .... *iv*

Suggestions for Using *Outdoor Action Games* .... *iv*

SECTION	*Grade Level*		
I. Operation Cooperation	*K–3*	*4–6*	*1*
Yarn It	X		*3*
Target Toss	X		*4*
Homemade P.E.	X	X	*5*
I Want My Blanky	X	X	*7*
Frisbee Golf	X	X	*8*
Crossfire	X	X	*9*
All Aboard	X	X	*10*
Free the Friz		X	*11*
Super Whooper		X	*13*
Ultimate Frisbee		X	*15*
Slam Dunk		X	*17*
Team Handball	X	X	*19*
II. Super Sweats	*K–3*	*4–6*	*21*
Task Card Challenges	X		*23*
Obstacle Course	X	X	*24*
Circuit Training Can Be Fun	X	X	*25*
Ball Tag Blast	X	X	*26*
Go for Twenty	X	X	*27*
Pin Ball Wizard	X	X	*29*
Runnin' Wild	X	X	*30*
The Wheel Deal	X	X	*32*
The Doctor Is In	X	X	*33*
Fun Run	X	X	*34*
Tire Tug	X	X	*35*
Rho-Sham-Bo and Go		X	*36*
Speedball		X	*37*
III. Lead-Up Games	*K–3*	*4–6*	*39*
. . . . . for Basketball *********************			*40*
Skill Development Stations for Basketball	X		*41*

	Col 1	Col 2	Page
Basketball Skills Stations		X	43
B-Ball Scramble	X		45
Pass 'n Run for Fun	X		46
Dribble Tag	X	X	47
A Blast with the Pass	X	X	48
Strive for Five	X	X	49
Four Corners B-Ball		X	50
Sections B-Ball		X	51
. . . . . for Softball **********************			52
Skill Development Stations for Softball	X		53
Softball Skills Stations		X	55
Bucket Chuck It	X		57
Skeeter	X		58
Around the Horn	X	X	59
Work-ups	X	X	60
Big Base Ball		X	62
Softball With a Wiggle		X	64
Boomer		X	66
Over the Line		X	67
. . . . . for Soccer ***************************			68
Skill Development Stations for Soccer	X		69
Soccer Skills Stations		X	71
Hoopla	X		73
Kickout	X		74
Footbag Frenzy	X	X	75
Four Corners Soccer	X	X	76
Side by Side Soccer	X	X	78
Alley Ball		X	79
Four-Way Pele		X	81
. . . . . for Volleyball *********************			82
Skill Development Stations for Volleyball	X		83
Volleyball Skills Stations		X	85
Control Yourself	X		87
Beachball Barrage	X		88
One Bounce Volleyball	X	X	89
Volleyback	X	X	90
"Tired Feet" Serving Practice		X	91
Ace Ball		X	93
Four-Way Volleyball		X	95

		K–3	4–6	
	. . . . . for Flag Football ********************			96
	Skill Development Stations for Football	X		97
	Football Skills Stations		X	99
	Hoop Scoot	X		101
	Throw the Pigskin and Grin	X		102
	Flag War	X	X	103
	100	X	X	104
	Vootball	X	X	105
	Four Down Sideways Football		X	107
	Throw and Go		X	109
	. . . . . Kickball Variations *****************			111
	One-Three-Five Stay Alive	X	X	112
	Teamwork Kickball	X	X	114
	Kickball-Basketball	X	X	116
	Three-Ball Do It All		X	118
	Kickball, and a Whole Lot More		X	120
	Super Hooper		X	122
IV.	**Something a Little Different**	*K–3*	*4–6*	125
	Video Highlight Delight	X	X	127
	Turn 'Em All Loose Duck Duck Goose	X	X	129
	Fun With Jugs	X	X	131
	Target Practice	X	X	133
	Frisbee Stations	X	X	134
	Up in the Air, On the Line, Knock It Down Frisbee	X	X	136
	Four-Way Disc Delight	X	X	138
	It's Hammer Time		X	140
	Juggling Is Catching		X	142
	Create a Game		X	144
V.	**Some Real A's**	*K–3*	*4–6*	147
	I'm Tired	X	X	149
	What a Drag	X	X	151
	Special Apparatus Relays	X	X	153
	Cooperative Group Relays	X	X	156
	Let's Get Together	X	X	158
	Know-and-Go Academic Relays	X	X	160
	Lead-Up Skill Relays	X	X	162
	H_2O A-Go-Go	X	X	164

VI. Academic Action	K–3	4–6		167
Animal Actions	X			169
Big Foot Relay	X			171
Toss and Answer	X	X		173
Yarn Art Patterns	X	X		175
Giant Tangram Creatures	X	X		177
Food for Survival	X	X		179
Arm Lock Math	X	X		181
Post-It Math	X	X		183
Grab + Race + Spell	X	X		185
Scramble to Win	X	X		186
Stop and Go Musical Hoops	X	X		188
Verb Actions	X	X		190
I Have ____, Who Has ____?	X	X		191
Science/Math Scavenger Hunt		X		193
Science Freeze Tag		X		195
Direction Run		X		196
Spider Web Definitions		X		198
State (or Country) Race		X		200
Rope Fences		X		202
Coordinate Frisbee (or Beanbag) Toss		X		204
Number Power Actions		X		206
VII. Reward Day Activities	**K–3**	**4–6**		209
..... *Reward Day Overview***************				211
Mini Carnival	X	X		212
Sports Smorgasbord	X	X		215
Van Gogh Where You Want To	X	X		216
Talent Explosion	X	X		217
Olympic Adventure	X	X		218
Melon Madness	X	X		220
Good Old-Fashioned Fun	X	X		222
It's Show Time	X	X		223
Obstacles Everywhere	X	X		224
Parents/Teachers/Students Reward Day	X	X		225
The Last Blast	X	X		226
APPENDIX				229
Equipment List				230
Suggestions for Obtaining Equipment				231
Equipment Request Letter				232

I OPERATION COOPERATION

The 12 activities in Section I help students develop cooperation skills
as well as physical skills.

YARN IT

Grades: K–3

Purposes: To improve balance and movement skills
To work on moving to a beat
To promote creativity and cooperation

Equipment: A piece of yarn or string for each person and a music source

Description: Cut a six- to ten-foot piece of yarn for each person. Make sure each participant has plenty of space for all activities.

Direct the participants to create a pathway with their yarn. Urge the children to use good balance and control as they walk along the pathway they design. Suggest various ways to move along the pathway (jump, hop, crawl, and so forth). Then, have them switch to someone else's pathway. Have the children work in pairs to create a pathway using both lengths of yarn. Then have participants work in groups of three or four to make one long, straight pathway. They can predict how many jumps or hops it will take to go from one end to the other. Add music and have individuals or small groups create dance steps that can be performed along the pathways. Have each group lead the others or perform their dance for other groups to end the activity.

Variations: (1) Form groups and set up some yarn path relays (hop down and back, wheelbarrow race with a partner, and so forth.) (2) Incorporate math or language into the activity by having children make numbers or letters with their yarn. Have participants work individually or in small groups to solve problems or answer questions by forming their yarn into the proper number or letter, and then have them move along the pathway in various ways.

TARGET TOSS

Grades: K–3

Purposes: To improve throwing accuracy
To promote cooperation

Equipment: A ball or beanbag and a hoop, tire, or piece of paper for each pair

Description: Have participants form pairs and stand about ten feet apart to begin. Each child places a hoop or tire on the ground near where they are standing. Make sure each pair has plenty of space.

Partners then take turns throwing the ball or beanbag in an attempt to make it land and remain inside the target. Score can be kept by allowing five points for a ball that lands inside the hoop, three points, for one that is touching the hoop, and one for a throw that is within a body length of the hoop. When mastery at a certain distance is achieved, partners can agree to move the hoops a bit farther apart.

Variations: (1) Have players play a round with their partner against another pair. In this version, use a "horseshoes" format where each person throws two balls, the opponent throws two, the score is totaled, and then the people on the other end do the same. Use the horseshoe scoring system. (2) Play a round where players must use their nondominant hand to throw. (3) Use bigger balls and play a soccer version of the game where players kick the ball toward the hoop rather than throw it. (4) Play a golf version by setting up a course with hoops and have players work their way around the course in pairs or foursomes.

HOMEMADE P.E.

Grades: K– 6

Purposes: To promote creativity
To promote enthusiasm and participation
To promote cooperation and camaraderie

Equipment: Whatever is necessary for the activities chosen

Description: Children get a lot of enjoyment and satisfaction from making something and being able to put it to use in a meaningful way. Begin the activity by having the participants make something and end the project by giving them the opportunity to use what they've made in a physical activity.

(1)   Participants can make or assemble simple kites and be allowed to run and play with them on a windy day.

(2)   Provide a long piece of rope and have each child cut a piece long enough to use as a jump rope. Have them tape the ends to prevent fraying. Give them a chance to put the jump ropes to immediate use.

(3)   Children can make drawings such as an animal, clown, or car and with a partner, can tape these drawings to a wall, and practice throwing as they attempt to hit certain parts of the drawings with a nylon ball or beanbag.

(4)   Individuals can draw a maze on a large piece of paper and challenge a partner to hop, jump, and so forth, as they attempt to find their way through the maze.

(5)   The leader can help the children make an ankle hop toy and allow the participants to practice during a physical education session.

(6)   Homemade hula-hoops can be fashioned out of plastic tubing and the leader can show the participants some variations that can be done with the new equipment.

(7)   Plastic jugs and bats can be made from liter and gallon plastic containers. Children can stuff old nylons with paper or pillow stuffing and play catch, or bat the balls back and forth.

Children will show a greater appreciation for equipment when given the chance to be a part of making it. Keep the homemade equipment around and bring it out periodically for Homemade P.E. sessions.

HOMEMADE P.E. *(Continued)*

Variations: (1) Have students do a *Homemade Homework* assignment where they make something with their parents and bring it to school to show the others how to play with it. Collect all the projects and devote a future P.E. session to the *Homemade Homework* activities. (2) Have students research handmade games and activities from other cultures. Have each person share their findings and allow some time for class participation.

I WANT MY BLANKY!

Grades: K–6

Purposes: To promote cooperation between members of a group
To improve quickness and coordination
To have a lot of fun

Equipment: An old blanket or sheet for every four to six players, and several balls of any type

Description: Blanket games can be played in any open area. Give each group of four to six players an old blanket or sheet, and a ball of some kind. Allow the groups some time to experiment with different techniques to propel the ball upward and catch it before it hits the ground, with their blanket.

Once the participants get a feel for sending the ball aloft and catching it, various games can be played. One activity is to have groups send the ball back and forth, increasing the distance as they improve their skills. Another game can be played in which one player throws the ball high or far, and groups coordinate their movements in an attempt to catch the ball. The group that catches three balls first gets to send one member to be the next thrower. When the groups become more skilled, teams can try to fling a ball so that it lands inside a bucket or box.

Any number of challenges can be developed using this fun set of activities. Participants will surely come up with some of their own ideas for new blanket games!

Variations: (1) Have the groups put several balls in their blankets and send them into the air to themselves, or to another group, to see how many they can catch. (2) Play *Basketball Blanketball*, where teams use a blanket to see who can fling their ball into the basket first, after "dribbling" the length of the court.

FRISBEE GOLF

Grades: K– 6

Purposes: To develop hand-eye coordination
To promote cooperation

Equipment: A Frisbee for each player

Description: The leader sets up a course of several "holes," which can be cones or objects labeled in some way, to serve as targets for the participants. Each pair or foursome should begin at a different hole so that everyone can start at the same time. Individual scores can be kept, or pairs can compete against each other as players attempt to advance their Frisbees to hit the target, the goal being to use the fewest number of total throws on each "hole." Players move through the course in numerical order until each person has made an attempt at each "hole" on the course.

Variations: (1) Rather than setting up a course, allow players to alternate choosing their own targets. In this version, one person simply calls out the object to be hit, and players are allowed to roam freely as they create their own "back nine"! (2) Players can alternate with special shots (behind the back toss, through the legs throw, nondominant hand toss, and so forth).

CROSSFIRE

Grades: K– 6

Purposes: To develop throwing accuracy
To promote cooperation and communication
To improve agility and dodging skills

Equipment: Several Nerf or stuffed nylon balls

Description: Divide the group into three equal teams. Place cones or markers in such a way that there are two sidelines about ten yards apart and an end line. Place a cone at the far end of the field from the end line, halfway between the two sidelines. Two of the teams form lines along opposite sidelines, facing each other, spaced so that they cover the entire sideline. The other team forms a single-file line at the middle of the end line. Distribute balls to several or all of the sideline players.

The object is for the players from the single-file line to run to the cone at the far end of the field and back without getting hit by a ball. Participants may jump, duck, roll, and dodge in any style they choose as the players from the sideline teams attempt to hit them with a ball (below the waist) as they make their way down and back. A point is scored for each successful trip to the cone, and another point can be scored on the way back. The game is played in relay fashion, so that one runner must tag the next teammate in line before s/he can begin to run toward the cone. When all the players have had a chance to run, the teams rotate in a clockwise fashion and the game continues.

Variations: (1) Have a new runner begin each time a teammate gets to the cone (which means two people are running at the same time). (2) Have runners make the trip down and back in pairs. (3) Have throwers use their non-dominant hand for a round. (4) Have throwers use different throwing styles to give runners more of a chance (underhand throw, between the legs, a football center snap style to "hike" the ball at runners, and so forth).

ALL ABOARD

Grades: K– 6

Purposes: To promote teamwork and cooperation
To provide an opportunity for continuous participation for all players
To improve kicking, catching, and throwing skills

Equipment: A kickball and four base markers

Description: Set up three bases and home plate, as in regular kickball. Divide the group into two equal teams. The defensive team takes the field in regular kickball positions. The offensive team forms a line behind the backstop well away from home plate.

One person from the offensive team is chosen to pitch to his/her team, and goes to the pitching mound with the ball. The first kicker stands behind home plate. The pitcher rolls the ball toward home plate, the kicker kicks the ball, and the wild train ride begins. All of the members of the kicker's team, including the pitcher, must run out to the kicker and form a train by latching on to each other, hands to waist, and travel as a unit around the bases, with the kicker leading the train. The object for the defensive team is to field the ball and toss it to a person at third base, then second, and finally to first before the last member of the train crosses home plate. If the train gets to home plate before the ball reaches first base, a run is scored. If the ball reaches first base before the train gets home, an out is recorded. When the defensive team accumulates three outs, the teams switch places, and the game continues.

Variations: (1) Have the defensive team pass the ball to each player to stop the train's progress rather than throw to bases. (2) Play a round with no foul balls; the defensive team must cover the entire field, and every kick is a live ball. (3) Use a different piece of equipment (Frisbee, football, and so forth).

FREE THE FRIZ

Grades: 4 – 6

Purposes: To promote cooperation

To provide an opportunity for all to participate, help form strategies, and get lots of exercise

Equipment: Several tires, hoops, lengths of rope, or any material that will serve to mark boundaries, and two Frisbees

Description: Place four or more tires (or other markers) on the ground on one side of one end of a playing field, and do the same on the other side of the same end of the field. Do the same thing at the other end of the field. Place a Frisbee in the center of one set of markers at each end of the field. The markers indicate the Frisbee and jail zones for each team. The field can be any size or shape.

Divide the players into two equal groups. Use cones, an existing field line, or any objects to mark the midline of the play area. Players begin each round by standing wherever they want on their side of the midline. Two guards should be assigned to the jail with two to protect the Frisbee for each team, and they should begin the round near the area they are to guard. Guards are not permitted to go inside the boundaries of the Frisbee zone; and it is a safety zone for opponents once they get inside.

On the signal to begin, players may go wherever they want to, whenever they want to. The object for each team is to cross through the opponents' side of the field and get their Frisbee, and then bring it back across the midline safely. When a player is on his/her side of the field s/he is in safe territory. Once a person crosses to the opponents' side of the field, if tagged, they must go to the jail. A teammate may come across to rescue others from jail. To do so, she/he must make it to the jail zone without being tagged. When this occurs, the person(s) that were set free and the person that freed them must walk back to their side of the field before making an offensive move toward the Frisbee again.

Once a person gets into the safety zone around the Frisbee, s/he must wait for an opportunity to grab the Frisbee and run without being tagged. Once a player takes off with the Frisbee, the scoring attempt becomes similar to *Ultimate Frisbee*, where the team attempting to score can use any combination of running and passing the Frisbee to advance it, with the goal being to safely cross the midline without being tagged while holding the Frisbee. Each time a team successfully brings the Frisbee across the midline, one point is scored. After each scoring attempt, regardless of whether or not it was successful, a new round begins.

FREE THE FRIZ *(Continued)*

Variations: (1) Play *Boppo Free the Friz,* where each player is armed with a Nerf or stuffed nylon ball and must hit opposing players with it to send them to jail, rather than tag them. (2) Take the equipment on a field trip or to a nearby park. The game is lots of fun to play in an area where there are trees and bushes to hide behind!

SUPER WHOOPER

Grades: 4 – 6

Purposes: To promote teamwork and cooperation
To improve hand-eye coordination, throwing, catching, and dodging skills

Equipment: One small rubber or dense foam rubber ball

Description: The game can be played on a football or soccer field, or cones can be used to mark a large rectangular area. Divide the group into two teams, and have one team at bat, with the other team spread out to cover the entire field.

The batting team assigns one of its players to be the pitcher. The batter can stand anywhere along the end line of the field to hit the ball. The batter strikes the pitched ball with a closed fist. The ball can be hit to any part of the field, and is in play as long as it bounces at least once inside the boundaries before rolling outside the sidelines. A caught fly ball is not an out.

The object for the batter is to run to the other end of the field and back, without getting hit (below the waist) by the ball. The batter can choose to remain across the endline at the far end of the field, rather than attempt to score on his/her own hit. A team can accumulate a maximum of two players in the safety zone at the far end of the field. When a third player hits the ball, one or both players must attempt to score from the safety zone. When a player crosses the line of the safety zone, s/he must attempt to score rather than return to safety.

The object for the team in the field is to retrieve the hit ball, and by relaying the ball through a series of tosses, get the ball close enough to the runner so that a hit can be made. A player may take a maximum of five steps with the ball before throwing it to a teammate. Once they hit a runner, the entire team must run as fast as it can toward the batting and scoring end of the field. If the player that got hit can retrieve the ball, chase down an opposing player, and hit the player before s/he crosses the line, his/her team remains at bat.

When a player is hit, and is unable to retrieve the ball and hit an opponent before s/he crosses the line, the teams switch places and the game continues.

Variations: (1) Play a round in which batters and fielders must use their nondominant hand. (2) Play a round in which a caught fly ball results in an automatic switch from offense to defense.

SUPER WHOOPER *(Continued)*

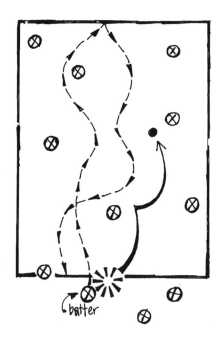

batter

ULTIMATE FRISBEE

Grades: 4 – 6

Purposes: Improve Frisbee throwing and catching skills
Develop offensive and defensive skills used in various sports
Promote teamwork and cooperation

Equipment: A Frisbee

Description: The "official" version of Ultimate Frisbee has seven members on each team, but the game can be played with more, or fewer players. Use existing lines on a football or soccer field, or mark off a large rectangle with cones. Have teams form lines outside opposite goal lines to begin the game.

The action begins with a "throw off," meaning a player from one team throws the disc toward the other team. When the disc is released, players from both teams may cross their goal lines. Players from the throwing team may not touch the disc before it is touched by the receiving team. The receiving team may catch the disc or let it fall to the ground. If the disc falls to the ground untouched, the receiving team is awarded possession. If a receiver attempts to catch the "throw off" and fails, the team that threw the disc gains possession. If the disc lands out of bounds, the receiving team may either choose to have the disc thrown again or take possession at the point where the disc crossed the sideline. If the disc goes over the goal line, possession begins in the nearest corner.

The object of the game is to advance the Frisbee across the opponents' goal line by using a series of throws and catches. A pass caught by a player in the end zone scores one point. Players must pass the disc to teammates; they cannot hand the disc to another player. Offensive players are not allowed to take steps once they control the Frisbee, however, they are allowed to pivot. Players must throw the Frisbee to another person within five seconds after gaining control of a pass. Defensive players are not allowed to make contact with offensive players or take or knock the Frisbee out of their hands. Only one player is allowed to guard the thrower. Defenders should be instructed to guard opponents from about three feet away. For any rule infraction, the disc is handed to the opponent and play resumes.

A disc dropped by the receiver without interference by the defender results in a turnover. The defensive team gains possession when a pass is incomplete, intercepted, or goes out of bounds. A turnover is put back into play by the player placing a pivot foot on the spot where the turnover occurred, and throwing the disc to a teammate. When the disc goes out of bounds, it is put back into play by a player placing one foot on the sideline at the point where it went out, and throwing the disc to another member of the team. When a team gains possession in the end zone they are defending, play is resumed by a player placing one foot on the goal line, and throwing the disc to a teammate.

ULTIMATE FRISBEE *(Continued)*

Variations: (1) If there are several players on each team, try using two or three Frisbees at the same time. (2) Try using different equipment with the same rules (a tennis ball, football, and so forth). (3) If there are several players, play a round where players must join hands, hold on to opposite sides of a tire or rag, or be connected in some other way, as they make their way around the field. (4) Once participants are experienced, have several smaller games going at the same time, and have players call their own violations.

SLAM DUNK

Grades: 4 – 6

Purposes: To promote teamwork
To improve throwing and catching skills
To build endurance and increase cardiovascular fitness

Equipment: One Nerf soccer ball, rubber playground ball or volleyball, and two bicycle tires or hoops

Description: Divide the group into two equal teams, with players from each team assigned to offensive and defensive positions similar to those used in soccer. A goal area for each team needs to be marked off with cones, or you may wish to use the existing lines on a football field. The size and shape of the goal area is flexible according to the grade level of the players, and depending on whether an offensive or defensive advantage is desired. You may wish to begin with a 20' by 20' area and experiment from there.

For each round, teams begin play on their half of the field until the ball is put into play, at which time offensive players move toward the opponents' goal, while defensive players stay back to defend their goal. The exception is that two players from each team begin play inside the goal area on the opponents' side of the field, holding a tire. One player for each team is assigned the defensive position inside the goal area, and that player's job is to follow the players holding the tire wherever they go and block or intercept scoring attempts. Play begins when the team with the ball makes the initial pass from one teammate to another.

The object is for a team to move the ball toward its own goal with a series of throws and catches and complete a successful scoring attempt. A one point goal is scored when the ball is thrown through a team's own tire, which is held by two of their teammates inside the goal area located on their opponents' end of the field. A three point goal is scored when a player manages to get close enough to "slam dunk" the ball through the tire.

A team maintains control of the ball as long as it successfully completes passes. A player can run for five steps, or until tagged, whichever comes first, and then must pass the ball to a teammate. A turnover occurs when the defensive team is able to intercept the ball or cause an incomplete pass. The ball is always "live," so that when a change of possession occurs, a player can pick up the loose ball and run immediately. Play does not stop until a goal is scored. When the ball goes out of bounds, the team in possession enters it with a pass. After a goal, players move back to their positions for the start of a new round, and the team just scored upon puts the ball into play.

SLAM DUNK *(Continued)*

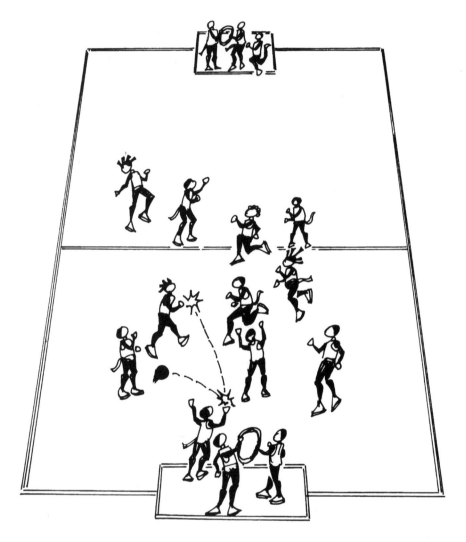

Variations: (1) Allow players to make forward progress until tagged by an opponent, thus dropping the five step rule. (2) To promote teamwork, make the requirement that each team member must handle the ball before a shot can be attempted. (3) End the game with a *Slam Dunk Competition,* where each participant gets to dazzle the crowd with hishe/her best dunk.

TEAM HANDBALL

Grades: 4 – 6

Purposes: To provide a strenuous aerobic workout
To improve coordination, agility, and endurance
To promote teamwork

Equipment: A ball that can be bounced and held in one hand by players

Description: Divide the group into two equal teams. The official version of the game calls for seven players on a team, including six field players and one goalie. The game can be played with additional field players. Mark sidelines and end lines for a large playing field. Mark a goal at each end approximately ten feet wide. Use chalk or markers to establish a goal area, penalty throw line, and free throw line as shown in the diagram.

Have teams spread out on their half of the field. At the beginning of the game, and after each goal, one team starts the action with a throw-on. The object is to move the ball toward the goal by running with it, or using a series of throws and catches until the ball can be thrown into the goal to score a point. Players are allowed to hold the ball for three seconds or three steps. After the first three steps, if the ball is dribbled, three more steps are allowed. Players are not allowed to kick the ball. Infractions result in a free throw for the opponents from the spot where the violation occurred.

Defensive players are allowed to closely guard and obstruct the progress of opponents. They are not allowed to hold, push, hit, or trip an opponent. A free shot is awarded from the spot where a foul occurs.

A throw-in occurs when the ball goes out of bounds. The person entering the ball must stand outside the line, and defenders must stand at least ten feet away. A goal throw takes place when the ball goes over the goal line, last touched by the offense. The goalie puts the ball back in play by throwing it from anywhere inside the goal area. A free throw takes place from the free throw line when a player enters the goal area or on any infraction by the goalie. The defensive players can help the goalie, but must stand at least ten feet away from the thrower. Offensive players must be behind the free throw line. A penalty throw occurs on severe fouls where the opponent stops a clear chance for a goal, or when a player throws the ball to their own goalie. In this case, all players except the thrower and goalie stand behind the free throw line. In the event of simultaneous possession, a referee's throw takes place, which is similar to a jump ball in basketball.

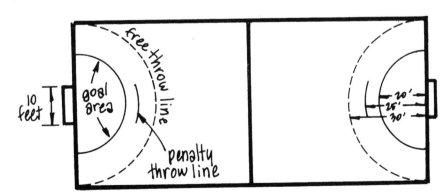

TEAM HANDBALL *(Continued)*

The goalie can move anywhere inside the goal area with the ball. The goalie cannot leave the goal area with the ball; however, the goalie can leave without the ball and become a field player. Once the goalie leaves the goal area, s/he cannot re-enter while possessing the ball. Field players cannot throw the ball to their own goalie.

Team Handball is a challenging game that requires endurance, skill, strategy, and teamwork. Once players become familiar with the game, they'll be hooked!

Variations: (1) If certain team members are not getting the ball very often, require that the ball be thrown to each member of the team before a shot can be taken. (2) If possible, once players know the game, break into smaller groups and play the official seven player version.

II SUPER SWEATS

The 13 SUPER SWEAT activities that follow help to develop quickness, agility, accuracy, and overall fitness.

TASK CARD CHALLENGES

Grades: K–3

Purposes: To promote concentration
To encourage participants to move in different ways
To work on moving to a beat

Equipment: Several task cards and a music source

Description: Make one set of cards with various movements written and illustrated so that all participants will be able to see (walk, run, roll, hop, bend, jump, and so forth.) Make another set of cards with different directional instructions (forward, backward, in a circle, sideways and so forth). The leader should have task cards, a music source, and a variety of musical choices to begin the activity. Have the participants spread out so that each person has plenty of space.

The leader chooses one of the movement cards and holds it up for all to see. Then the leader picks a card with a direction on it and shows the group. The leader starts the music, and as soon as each person can figure out how to combine the movement with the direction and the music, s/he begins to move. Allow plenty of time for each combination to make sure all participants have an adequate opportunity to complete each round successfully.

Variations: (1) The leader can use a drum or anything to make a beat and have participants follow various patterns (hop forward on beats 1, 2, 3, 4, and jump sideways on beats 6, 7, 8, 9, and so forth). (2) Choose a participant to select the cards and act as the leader for each round. (3) Incorporate various pieces of equipment into the activity and change the task cards (use a ball and make cards that would result in combinations such as walk forward and bounce the ball, hop sideways and throw the ball up and catch it, and so forth).

OBSTACLE COURSE

Grades: K– 6

Purposes: To increase quickness, speed, endurance, agility, coordination, and overall fitness in a fun and challenging way

Equipment: Hoops, tires, cones, boxes, rope, and any objects that can be incorporated to make the desired course

Description: The leader needs to gather the desired equipment and design and lay out a challenging obstacle course. Hoops, cones, boxes, rope and other equipment can be arranged to make a course where participants must run, climb, crawl, jump, hop, pull, push, and use a variety of other movements in order to complete the activity.

The course can be set up to accommodate one person at a time, in which case a stopwatch may be used to determine winners, or if time allows, individuals may go through the course two or more times to see if they can improve their time. The course can also be constructed in such a way that two people can go through together in a race toward the finish line.

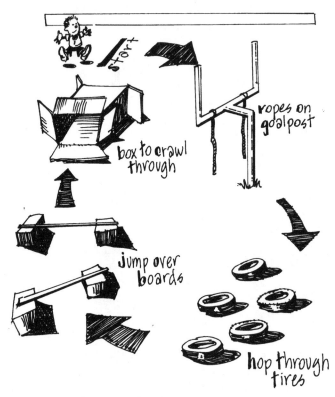

Variations: (1) Form teams and use a relay format. (2) Incorporate additional tasks such as pull-ups, bar dips, and so forth, to make it a *Circuit Training Obstacle Course.* (3) Allow the participants to help design new courses by changing or adding new challenges to the course.

CIRCUIT TRAINING CAN BE FUN

Grades: K– 6

Purposes: To improve overall fitness while having fun
To provide an opportunity for continuous participation for all players

Equipment: Whatever is necessary to complete the activities included in the course

Description: The leader needs to design and lay out a course that includes the desired activities. A series of fitness movements, intermingled with some fun and challenging skill activities will inspire and encourage participants to complete the course to the best of their abilities.

Examples of some fitness stations would be areas set up for push-ups, sit-ups, pull-ups, jump rope, stretching, balancing, and so forth. Examples of activities that can be intermingled as part of the course would be stations where participants shoot ten free throws, kick a field goal, throw a ball at a tire tied to a backstop, hit a tennis ball against a wall, or dribble a soccer ball ten yards, and so forth.

Assign people to begin at certain stations, and establish a pattern of rotation to be followed by the participants as they work their way through the course. The object is for each person to attempt each activity to the best of his/her ability, then run or jog to the next station, and continue until s/he has completed each activity on the course.

Variations: (1) Use the activity as a daily fitness challenge, time participants each day, and have them work toward reducing their time. (2) Have participants form pairs and assist each other as they work their way through the course. (3) Allow participants to create new activities and come up with several new courses.

BALL TAG BLAST

Grades: K– 6

Purposes: To improve throwing accuracy
To increase quickness, agility, and dodging skills
To provide an opportunity for continuous participation by all players

Equipment: One or more Nerf or stuffed nylon balls

Description: Mark boundaries for an area large enough for the group to have plenty of room to run in all directions. Have players scatter about the play area, and choose one person to begin the game with the ball. The object is for the person with the ball to chase other players until s/he gets close enough to hit someone with the ball. When a player gets hit by the ball s/he becomes the new chaser.

To maintain interest and add excitement and enthusiasm to the game, the leader can call out specific body parts to be hit by the person throwing the ball. Start with a round of Knee and Flee, switch to Toe and Go, try Bun and Run, or whatever version the leader or players can dream up!

Variations: (1) Have at least two, or several people chase and throw at the same time. (2) Give everyone a ball to start, and play an elimination round where everyone is pursuing everyone else, with the goal being to be the last person hit. In this version, when a player is hit s/he must walk to the edge of the play area and watch until a new round begins. (3) Have the players make all throws with their nondominant hand for a round.

GO FOR TWENTY

Grades: K– 6

Purposes: To provide a strenuous aerobic activity
To provide an opportunity for continuous action for all participants
To improve quickness, agility, and stamina
To promote cooperation

Equipment: Twenty tennis balls, a flag for each player plus a few extras, and some cones, rope, or markers

Description: Mark boundaries for a rectangular field approximately thirty yards wide and fifty yards long. Use cones, rope, or markers to lay out a circle about fifteen feet in diameter toward the end line of each side of the field. Place ten tennis balls at the center of each circle. Place a few flags across the midline of the field. Divide the group into two equal teams. Have teams spread out on opposite sides of the field with some players back to defend their circle zone. Each person should be wearing one or two flags.

The object is for players to make their way to the opponents' circle zone without having their flag pulled, pick up a ball, and run back to their side of the field and place the ball inside their own circle. Once inside the circle, players are safe and can wait for a good opportunity to make a run for it. When a player's flag is pulled, s/he becomes frozen in that spot until a teammate takes one of the extra flags from the midline and runs safely to the frozen player. When a rescue is made, the players run back to their own side of the field, each holding one end of the flag as they go. When a player has possession of a ball at the time his/her flag is pulled, the ball must be returned to the circle zone. Pulled flags should be placed across the midline of the field for future use.

The action does not stop until all twenty balls are in one team's circle zone. Therefore, the game can be played until one team gets all twenty, and then another round begins, or it can be played for a certain period of time, in which case the team with the most balls in their circle when time expires wins.

GO FOR TWENTY (Continued)

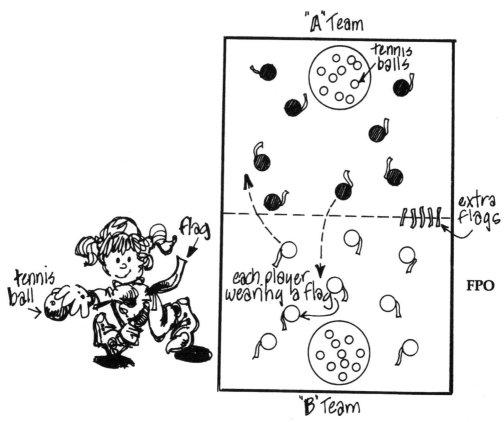

Variations: (1) Use different equipment with the same basic format (put basketballs in the circles and have players dribble on their way, or use jump ropes and require people to skip rope to their side of the field). (2) Use the same equipment but change the method of locomotion (players must hop, run backwards, sidestep, and so forth on their way to the circle and back). (3) The game can be played using the one-or two-hand touch system if flags are not available.

PIN BALL WIZARD

Grades: K– 6

Purposes: To provide practice in any skills desired
To increase the level of involvement for all participants
To encourage development of strategies

Equipment: Depending on the version played, a soccer ball, football, or kickball, and some cones or pins

Description: Set up a rectangular field approximately the size of a football or soccer field. Place several cones or pins randomly throughout the field. Divide the group into two equal teams, and have teams assume regular soccer positions on opposite sides of the field.

Regular soccer rules apply; however, points can be scored by knocking pins over as well as by kicking a goal. One point is awarded a team when a player manages to kick the ball and knock over one of the pins, and three points are scored on a successful shot at the goal. The leader can follow the ball and reset pins that have been knocked over, or players not involved in the play can set them back up as the action continues.

The game should serve to encourage players to stay in their positions, because all pin areas must be guarded, as well as the goal areas. Several different versions of the activity can be used depending on the skill development desired, so be sure to check the variations listed below.

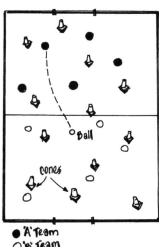

Variations: (1) Use the same idea in a game of *Throw and Go* (*see* Table of Contents). In this version, the player with the ball can run by a pin and knock it over with the football as s/he moves upfield. One point is awarded for a pin knocked down, and three for getting the ball into the opponents' end zone. (2) Play a game of basketball using the same system. The player with the ball must continue to dribble as s/he passes by pins and attempts to knock them down with his/her free hand. One point is recorded for knocking down a pin, and three are scored for a basket. (3) Play a game of kickball with cones set up just out of the base paths between each base. The runner can pass by the pin, or s/he can try to detour out of the base line, knock over a pin, and run to the next base. Record one point for each pin knocked down, and two points for crossing home plate.

RUNNIN' WILD

Grades: K–6

Purposes: To provide an opportunity for continuous activity by all participants
To improve running, dodging, and chasing skills
To provide a strenuous aerobic workout
To promote cooperation and strategy development

Equipment: Several hoops or old bike tires, an equal number of tennis balls or any substitute objects, and flags for all players if desired

Description: Mark boundaries and a midline for a rectangular field approximately the size of a soccer or football field. Scatter several hoops or tires randomly on both sides of the field, and place a tennis ball inside each one. Divide the group into two equal teams and have one team line up along the midline, while the other team scatters to cover all areas of their side of the field. Players can be given flags to wear, or a one-hand touch system can be used.

On the signal to begin, all players make a run toward their opponents' end line. The object is for the runners to make it across their opponents' end line without getting tagged or having their flag pulled. One point is scored for each person that makes the trip safely. In addition, five points are recorded for each player that manages to pick up a tennis ball along the way and still makes it across the line without getting caught by an opponent.

After each trip, the team total is recorded and teams reset the tennis balls and return to starting positions, alternating each time as runners and taggers. The game can be played for a certain time period, or a certain point total to be reached can be established.

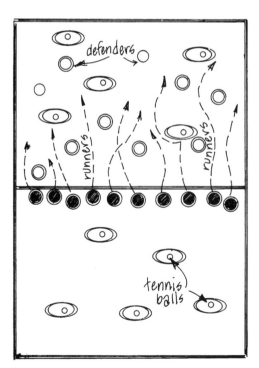

RUNNIN' WILD *(Continued)*

Variations: (1) To make the reset process more fun, players can be awarded an extra point if they are able to throw the ball from the end line and make it land inside the hoop. (2) Change the objects in the tires and the task to be accomplished with them (put jump ropes inside and have players jump rope as they run to the end line, use volleyballs and have them keep the ball aloft with bumps and sets as they go, use basketballs and have them dribble, and so forth). (3) Make the job harder for the taggers (have them hold hands and travel in pairs, or have them throw Nerf balls at runners and hit them instead of tagging them, and so forth).

THE WHEEL DEAL

Grades: K– 6

Purposes: To provide an opportunity for continuous activity by all participants
To provide a strenuous aerobic workout
To improve quickness, agility, dodging, and chasing skills

Equipment: Several hoops or old tires and several tennis balls or similar objects

Description: Place several hoops or tires in a large circle, with one hoop in the center containing several tennis balls. Assign two to eight people as guards, and have all the other players stand inside the hoops that form the perimeter of the playing field.

The object is for players to run to the hoop and get one of the tennis balls without being tagged by one of the guards. The perimeter hoops are safety zones, but players can only stay inside a hoop for five seconds before they must run to a different hoop or make an attempt to get a tennis ball. No more than three players are allowed inside a hoop at a time.

When a player manages to get a tennis ball, s/he tosses it to the leader and gets a free walk back to a perimeter tire. The game continues until all the tennis balls have been taken from inside the hoop. A new set of guards is chosen and another round begins.

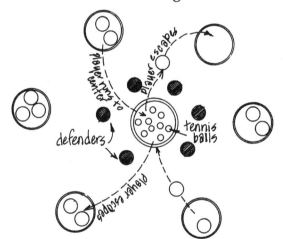

Variations: (1) Add a task to be accomplished when a ball is taken (toss it into a bucket, throw it through a hoop, and so forth). If the person is unsuccessful, the ball goes back into the hoop. (2) Have players change roles each time someone is tagged outside the hoops instead of waiting until all tennis balls are taken. (3) Play a musical version where all players caught outside the hoops when the music stops are the new guards. (4) Play the game using a very large field. (5) Break into smaller groups and have several games going at the same time. (6) Have players perform a task after being caught before returning to a perimeter tire (for example, make two free throws, or dribble a soccer ball around some cones, and so forth). (7) Play an equal teams version. In this case add a jail for players that get caught, and have their teammates rescue them before they can return to a hoop. Teams switch when all balls have been taken from the hoop.

THE DOCTOR IS IN

Grades: K– 6

Purposes: To improve throwing accuracy
To improve agility and dodging skills
To provide an opportunity for all players to participate continuously

Equipment: Several Nerf balls or stuffed nylon balls, and two "healing sticks" (for example, whiffle bats, rolled up magazine, padded yardsticks)

Description: Cone off a large rectangle or square, or use existing lines for boundaries, and mark a midline. Divide the group into two equal teams, and have teams scatter about the field on opposite sides of the midline. One person for each team is chosen to be The Doctor, and is given the "healing stick." The Doctor for each team begins the game by standing behind a wall of teammates, as far away from the opponents as possible. The Doctor has the power to heal injured teammates by touching them with the "healing stick."

The object of the game is to eliminate all the players on the opposing team. Once a person is hit by a ball (leader should indicate legal shots, below the shoulders, below the waist, and so forth) s/he must fall to the ground and pretend to be injured. The Doctor must make his/her way to the injured teammate and touch the person with the "healing stick," at which time the player can get back up and continue to participate. The trick is for one team to hit The Doctor, who cannot heal him/herself or anyone else after being hit, and then finish off the remaining players. Once all the players from one team have been eliminated the opponents score one point, the players reset, and another round begins.

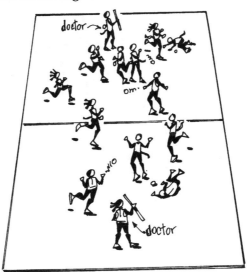

Variations: (1) Introduce an "instant death" ball (different size or color). When a player is hit by the special weapon, s/he cannot be healed by the doctor. (2) Play a round of *Kamikaze* where players can cross into the opponents' territory and attempt a suicidal attack on The Doctor. (3) To keep all players involved, after a team's doctor has been eliminated, allow all eliminated players to sit up and block balls that are aimed at the remaining players on their team. (4) Indicate special places the ball must contact a person to be considered a legal hit (for instance, feet only, ankle to knee, and so forth).

FUN RUN

Grades: K– 6

Purposes: To increase running stamina
To promote teamwork
To improve kicking skills
To provide fun aerobic exercise

Equipment: One ball that can be kicked

Description: This game can be played in any large open space. Divide the group into two teams, and have each team form a single-file line. The ball is given to the front player of one of the teams.

The game begins when the person with the ball kicks it as far as s/he can in any direction, and begins to run around his/her entire team as fast as possible. The kicker keeps circling his/her team until the opposing team completes its task. The object for the other team is to begin running after the ball as soon as it is kicked. The first player to reach the ball picks it up, and the remaining players form a single-file line behind that player as they arrive. A point is scored for the kicking team for each complete trip the kicker can make around his/her team before the other team is in place.

The person that controls the ball after the previous kick becomes the new kicker. S/he kicks the ball and the process is repeated. The action never stops in this fast-paced game, and participants will enjoy a good workout.

Variations: (1) Add an additional task to the challenge (person circling the team must do three pushups after each complete trip, and so forth). (2) Play the game with boundaries to focus on placement of kicks, and to decrease the amount of running if desired.

TIRE TUG

Grades: K– 6

Purposes: To increase upper body and leg strength
To provide vigorous exercise
To improve balance and agility
To have a lot of fun

Equipment: An old bicycle tire wrapped with padding

Description: Wrap an old bike tire with towels or strips of material for padding. Use existing lines on a football or soccer field, or use cones to mark end lines ten to twenty yards apart, and a midline between the two end lines. Divide the group into two teams, and have them form lines at opposite ends of the field. Players can be assigned numbers, or a *Four Corners Soccer* (*see* Table of Contents) format may be used.

The game begins when the leader calls out a number, or blows a whistle if the Four Corners format is being used. On the signal to begin, the appropriate players run toward the tire and grab hold of it as soon as they get there (the game can also be started with players holding the tire in the middle of the playing field). The object is for players to get the tire back to, and across, their own end line. Players pull, tug, yank, or run with the tire in an attempt to move it closer to their end line. Players may not trip or push opponents at any time. The leader should monitor the action closely to ensure that players do not become too rough during the game. A point is scored when a team pulls the tire completely across their goal line successfully.

This variation of Tug-O-War is a lot of fun and provides participants with a vigorous upper and lower body workout.

Variations: (1) Call multiple numbers, or doubles or triples if using the Four Corners format, to increase the number of participants per round. (2) Add an additional challenge to the game by allowing a player from the winning team on each round to earn an extra point by successfully tossing the tire around a cone placed several feet away.

RHO-SHAM-BO AND GO

Grades: 4 – 6

Purposes: To promote quick thinking and reactions
To improve quickness and agility
To promote cooperation

Equipment: Some cones or markers if existing lines are not available, and flags if desired

Description: Divide the group into two equal teams, and have the teams face each other at the center of the playing field. Mark off a rectangular field approximately thirty yards wide and fifty yards long.

The rock, scissors, and paper gestures are used to determine who chases whom. The object is for the team that wins the "Rho-Sham-Bo" to chase and tag as many of the players from the other team as they can before the opponents can cross the line at the end of their own side of the field. Teams huddle before each round to agree on which symbol they will show the other team. Both teams come towards the center line, and each participant decides how close to the opponents s/he wants to stand. Players pound their fists in unison, and on the third time show the symbol that was agreed upon by the team. All members from the same team must show the same symbol. If both teams show the same symbol, they rehuddle and try again. As soon as individuals figure out who won (rock beats scissors, paper beats rock, and scissors beat paper) the winners chase and tag as many people as they can, while the others run and dodge to get across their end line without being tagged.

When a person gets tagged, s/he must join the other team. Play continues until all players end up on the same team, and then another round begins with equal teams.

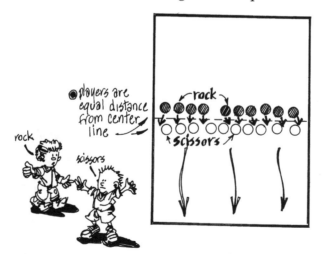

Variations: (1) Make up different symbols from various subject areas to use instead of using rock, paper, and scissors (for instance, triangle, square, and rectangle: triangle beats rectangle; rectangle beats square; square beats triangle). (2) Add a task for people that get tagged each round (they must join hands and run or hop to the end line and back, or must complete five successful group jump rope moves, and so forth).

SPEEDBALL

Grades: 4 – 6

Purposes: To improve throwing strength and accuracy
To improve catching skills
To increase quickness and agility
To promote cooperation
To provide an opportunity for continuous participation by all players

Equipment: One or more Nerf soccer balls, or any nonthreatening ball as a substitute

Description: The game can be played on any surface. Use cones to mark off a rectangle about the size of a volleyball court (30' by 60') and mark a midline across the play area.

Divide the players into two equal groups. Players spread out evenly on their side of the court. Each team needs to assign two shaggers to play outside of the opponents' end line. The object of the game is to hit opponents with the ball until one team's players have all been eliminated. If a player catches a thrown ball s/he is not eliminated, and the same holds true if a ball bounces before hitting a player. The leader should specify what will count as a legal hit before play begins (below the shoulders, below the waist, and so forth).

This is a nonelimination game in that when a player gets hit by the ball s/he continues in the game by walking outside the court to the opponents' end line and becomes a shagger. Shaggers retrieve balls that leave the court and are permitted to throw them at the opponents. As the game progresses, there will be more shaggers and less people inside the court, until finally all the players from one team are eliminated. When this occurs, a point is scored, and players return to their original positions to begin a new round.

SPEEDBALL *(Continued)*

Variations: (1) Allow shaggers to move around to the sides of the court so that they are on all three sides of the opponents' end of the court. (2) Use at least two, or several balls at the same time. (3) Have players throw with their nondominant hand for a round. (4) Play the game with a volleyball net suspended across the middle of the court. Players must throw the ball over the net. This version makes it much easier for people to dodge the ball.

LEAD-UP GAMES

for

— BASKETBALL —
— SOFTBALL —
— SOCCER —
— VOLLEYBALL —
— FLAG FOOTBALL —

plus
— KICKBALL Variations —

This section includes 52 games that help to develop the physical skills and teamwork needed for the sports listed above.

BASKETBALL

Lead-Up Games

SKILL DEVELOPMENT STATIONS FOR BASKETBALL

Grades: K–3

Purposes: To provide opportunities for primary grade children to develop skills that can later be used in basketball

Equipment: Several basketballs or playground balls, some cones, and a few hoops or tires

Description: Divide the participants into five equal groups. Assign each group to a different station, and establish a rotation pattern to be followed when the signal to switch is given. Set up the stations so that participants have adequate space for each activity, and in such a way that the leader and helpers can monitor all stations efficiently.

Station #1) DRIBBLING: Place enough hoops or tires on the ground so that each person has his/her own. Have the participants attempt to dribble continuously while making the ball bounce inside the hoop each time.

Station #2) DRIBBLE AND RUN: Have participants practice controlling their dribble while they move. Have people dribble down and back to a cone while walking or running.

Station #3) PASSING AND CATCHING: Have participants work in pairs to practice passing accuracy and catching skills. Participants stand a few feet apart and take turns using direct passes or bounce passes to send the ball toward their partner. When pairs demonstrate mastery at a certain distance, they can each take a step backwards and continue.

Station #4) DEFENSE: Have the members of the group form a circle, with one person in the middle. Circle players play "keep away" using two-handed passes, while the person in the middle uses quick movements to try to get the ball. After ten passes, or when the person in the middle gets the ball, a new person should move to the middle, so that all participants get a chance to practice defense.

Station #5) SHOOTING: Place hoops near a wall and have participants practice a two-handed shooting motion as they attempt to make the ball land inside the hoop, then retrieve the ball, and repeat the movement. As people become more skilled, they can move farther back.

SKILL DEVELOPMENT STATIONS
FOR BASKETBALL *(Continued)*

Variations: (1) As participants become more skilled, increase the difficulty of the activity by adding an extra challenge (set up a course that requires more skill for station #2, have participants shoot into a barrel or real basketball hoop for station #5, have them use their nondominant hand for station #1 and so forth). (2) Create variations for each station (for instance, circle players must dribble once before passing at station #4, change the requirements at station #1 to alternating one dribble inside the hoop, then one outside the hoop, place a hoop between pairs at station #3 and have them attempt to make a bounce pass where the ball lands inside the hoop).

BASKETBALL SKILLS STATIONS

Grades: 4 – 6

Purposes: To provide practice in all basketball skills
To increase overall coordination and agility

Equipment: Four basketballs

Description: Divide the players into four equal groups. Designate an area for each activity, and assign a group to each area. Establish a rotation pattern to be followed by groups when the signal to switch is given.

This activity can be used for one or several entire physical education periods, or it can be used to begin each basketball session prior to the actual game.

Station #1) DRIBBLING: Have players form a line at one end of a basketball court. Players are to dribble from one end of the court to the other using their dominant hand, and then dribble back using their nondominant hand.

Station #2) PASSING: Divide the players into two equal groups. Each person lines up facing a partner, about ten to fifteen feet apart. Participants pass the ball back and forth using a variety of passing techniques (chest pass, bounce pass, baseball pass, and so forth). The receiving player should practice stepping toward the ball to receive the pass.

Station #3) SHOOTING/REBOUNDING: Divide players into two equal groups. Half the players form a line at the intersection of the sideline and the half court line, while the other group does the same on the other side of the court. The ball is given to the first person in one of the lines. The person with the ball dribbles toward the basket and shoots a layup or an outside shot. The first person in the other line runs toward the basket as the shooter begins to dribble, gets into rebounding position, rebounds the ball, and passes the ball to the next player in the shooting line. Each player returns to the end of the opposite line so that everyone gets several turns at each position.

Station #4) FREE THROWS/REBOUNDING: Have players take positions around the key, with one player at the free throw line. The person on the line shoots a free throw, while the other players work for position and attempt to get the rebound. After each shot, players rotate in a clockwise fashion so that each person gets several chances at each position.

BASKETBALL SKILLS STATIONS *(Continued)*

Variations: (1) Change the dribbling station to *Dribble Tag* (*see* Table of Contents). (2) Change the passing station to *Blast with the Pass* (*see* Table of Contents). (3) Change the shooting/rebounding station by allowing the person from the rebounding line to defend the shooter rather than just rebounding the ball. (4) Change the free throw/rebounding station by having the player that gets the rebound go directly to the free throw line, and allow the shooter to stay until an attempt is missed.

B-BALL SCRAMBLE

Grades: K–3

Purposes: To improve basketball dribbling skills
To improve basketball shooting skills

Equipment: Several basketballs or playground balls, and a box or bucket

Description: Place a box or bucket containing several balls at the center of a basketball court. Have the players scatter themselves so that all areas of the court are covered.

The leader begins the action by tossing the balls in all directions as fast as possible. The object for the players is to catch or retrieve the balls, dribble to the bucket, and place the balls back inside as quickly as possible. The leader controls the pace as the players try to fill the bucket. To finish the game, the leader can let the children win by allowing the bucket to be filled.

Variations: (1) Mark a circle around the bucket with rope or chalk and have players shoot the ball into the bucket rather than simply placing it back in. (2) Have players dribble to the nearest hoop and make one shot before they dribble to the bucket to put the ball back. (3) Let one of the children be the leader for a round. (4) Play a round where players must dribble with their nondominant hand at all times.

PASS 'N RUN FOR FUN

Grades: K–3

Purposes: To improve basketball passing skills
To increase hand-eye coordination and quickness
To improve catching skills

Equipment: A basketball or large foam ball for each group

Description: Have players form groups of five to ten. Each group needs to form a circle with players several feet apart. One person is chosen to begin with the ball.

The person with the ball begins the action by passing it to one of the other players in the group. As soon as the ball is passed, the person that started with the ball begins running around the outside of the circle. The players in the circle attempt to pass the ball to each person in the group before the runner can run once around the circle and get back to his/her original spot. Circle players cannot pass to a person standing right next to them. Players take turns as the person that begins the action, and the game continues.

Variations: (1) Have players work on specific passes each round (such as bounce pass, chest pass, and so forth). (2) Have the runner dribble a ball as s/he runs around the circle. (3) Have the runner dribble to a basket, make one shot, and come back while the players pass the ball three times each.

DRIBBLE TAG

Grades: K– 6

Purposes: To improve basketball dribbling skills
To improve agility and quickness

Equipment: One or more basketballs

Description: The game can be played on a basketball court, or on any paved area. If played on a basketball court, the boundaries can either be the whole court, or half the court. On a paved surface other than a basketball court, cones can be used to mark the boundaries for a large area.

One participant is chosen to be the dribbler of the basketball. The other players scatter themselves within the boundaries. When the signal to begin is given, the person with the ball dribbles anywhere within the boundaries, while attempting to tag another player. The dribbler must be in control of the ball when the tag is made if it is to count. Participants must use their agility and quickness to avoid being tagged. When the dribbler tags someone while successfully controlling his/her dribble, the person tagged becomes the new dribbler, and the game continues.

Variations: (1) Have dribblers use their nondominant hand to dribble. (2) Break into smaller groups and have several games going on at the same time. (3) Have two or three people assigned as dribblers. (4) Incorporate additional basketball skills by having those being chased use defensive side-step or back–pedaling movements. (5) For expert dribblers, make the task harder by having them balance a beanbag on their head while dribbling and chasing others. (6) For young players, simply have them bounce the ball once and catch it every few steps.

A BLAST WITH THE PASS

Grades: K–6

Purposes: To improve basketball passing skills
To improve quickness and defensive skills

Equipment: One or more basketballs

Description: Have participants form a large circle, standing two to four feet apart. One person is chosen to be in the center of the circle. A circle player is given the ball, and begins the game by using a chest pass to get the ball to another player that is part of the circle. A pass cannot be made to the player standing right next to the passer. The object for circle players is to make a successful pass to another circle player.

The object for the player inside the circle is to intercept a pass before it is received by the circle player for which it is intended. When a player intercepts a pass, s/he changes places with the player that threw the pass, and the game continues.

Variations: (1) Use more than one ball. (2) Allow two or more players inside the circle. (3) Break into smaller groups and have several games going at once. (4) To make it easier for the person inside the circle, have players change places when a ball is touched or intercepted. (5) Have a "Globetrotters" round where all passes must be between the legs or behind the back.

STRIVE FOR FIVE

Grades: K– 6

Purposes: To provide practice in basketball passing and defensive skills
To promote teamwork and cooperation

Equipment: A basketball

Description: Divide the group into two equal teams. Players from both teams scatter about the entire basketball court. Each player should choose or be assigned someone from the opposing team to guard when their team is playing defense. One team is chosen to begin with the ball, and a member of that team stands outside the sideline at midcourt ready to enter the ball to a teammate.

The object is for a team to complete five consecutive passes without letting the defensive team take the ball away. When a team completes five successive passes in a row, a point is scored, and the other team takes the ball out of bounds and attempts to do the same thing. If the defensive team takes the ball away before the opponent can complete five passes, they begin passing immediately without having to inbound the ball from the sideline. When the ball goes out of bounds, it is considered a stolen pass, and the defensive team takes possession. Fouls are called as in regular basketball, and the ball changes possession after each foul called.

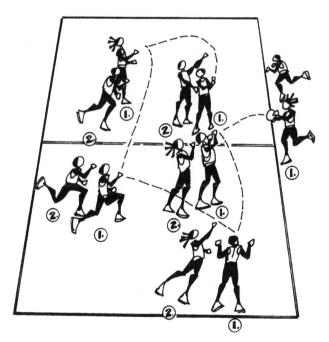

Variations: (1) Allow the team to shoot at the nearest basket after completing five passes. If the shot goes in, an additional point is scored and the ball is awarded to the defensive team. If the shot is missed, either team can gain control by getting the rebound, and play continues. (2) Have a "Globetrotters" round, where behind the back or between the legs passes count as two passes. (3) Once players know the game, break into smaller groups and have several games going at the same time.

FOUR CORNERS B-BALL

Grades: 4 – 6

Purposes: To provide practice and develop all basketball skills
To promote teamwork and cooperation

Equipment: One basketball

Description: Divide the players into two equal teams. Players line up along the end lines and sidelines of the court as shown below. One half of Team O lines up on half of one end line, around the corner and along half of one sideline. The other half of Team O does the same thing along the opposite end line and sideline. Team X spreads their players in the same manner along opposite end lines and sidelines. The leader indicates the offensive basket for each team.

The leader signals to participants by holding up one, two, or three fingers to indicate the number of court players for each round. For example, if the leader holds up one finger, only one player from the beginning of each of the four lines (front of line is person nearest the basket) would be a court player for that round. The leader blows a whistle to begin the action, and enters the ball by tossing the ball into the air, toward one participant, bouncing it against the backboard, and so forth, and players scramble for the first possession. Regular basketball rules apply once play begins.

The goal for each team is to score a basket on their offensive end of the court. Sideline players become involved whenever the ball would normally go out of bounds. When the ball is controlled by a sideline player, s/he may pass it to a teammate that is a court player. Thus, the action does not stop until a basket is scored. After a basket is scored, the court players feed back to the end of their line, and new players rotate up to become the court players for the next round.

Variations: (1) Allow court players to pass to their sideline teammates at any time during the action. (2) Allow sideline players to shoot the ball, and count their shots as three point baskets.

SECTIONS B-BALL

Grades: 4 – 6

Purposes: To improve one-on-one offensive and defensive skills
To provide practice in throwing and receiving passes

Equipment: One or more basketballs

Description: Use chalk to divide the basketball court into equal sections. There should be one section for each pair of participants. Number the sections as shown below. Divide the group into two equal teams. Players number off, and are assigned to the corresponding section on the court. There should be one player from each team in each section of the court. The leader indicates which is the offensive basket for each team.

The object is for each team to attempt to work the ball toward its own basket and score. Shots can be made from anywhere, but players should be encouraged to shoot only from sections close to the basket. Regular basketball rules apply, except that players must remain in their section during play. Players may move about freely inside their section to get offensive or defensive position. Offensive players may dribble and pivot inside the section before passing the ball to a teammate. When the ball goes out of bounds, the player from that section who is awarded possession enters it from outside the court by passing it to a teammate in a nearby section. After each basket, players rotate to the next section so that all participants get to play each position.

Variations: (1) If two or more courts are available, have several games going at the same time to allow for larger sections for each pair of players. (2) In a one court situation, use two basketballs at the same time. (3) Have one or more players from each team positioned outside the court as "safety valves." They can receive passes and dribble to a different section to re-enter the ball.

SOFTBALL

Lead-Up Games

SKILL DEVELOPMENT STATIONS FOR SOFTBALL

Grades: K–3

Purposes: To provide opportunities for primary grade students to develop skills that can later be used in softball

Equipment: Several foam rubber balls, playground balls, tennis balls, or beanbags

Description: Divide the participants into five equal groups. Assign each group to a different station, and establish a rotation pattern to be followed when the signal to switch is given. Set up the stations so that participants have adequate space for each activity, and in such a way that the leader and helpers can monitor all stations efficiently.

Station #1) THROWING: Tape several pieces of paper or posters to the wall and have each person at the station throw a ball at his/her target, retrieve the ball, and repeat the process. Have the participants take a step back each time they hit the target three times in a row.

Station #2) THROWING AND CATCHING: Have participants form pairs and work on throwing accuracy and catching skills as they throw a ball back and forth. Have them move farther apart when they demonstrate mastery at each distance.

Station #3) THROWING AND CATCHING GROUNDERS: Participants work in pairs as they use an underhand or overhand throwing motion to roll the ball toward their partner. The person receiving the ball squats and uses both hands to catch the ball.

Station #4) THROWING AND CATCHING FLIES: Have participants form pairs and practice throwing and catching fly balls. Instruct them to begin by standing very close to each other as they take turns throwing the ball a few feet in the air toward their partner, who attempts to catch the ball using both hands. When participants demonstrate mastery at a close distance, they should move farther apart and throw the ball a bit higher.

Station #5) HITTING: Use a plastic or foam bat and ball to have participants practice hitting from a batting apparatus (T-Ball stand). Have all participants hit and retrieve their own balls, or have one person hit while the others in the group retrieve the ball and throw it back to the hitter.

SKILL DEVELOPMENT STATIONS FOR SOFTBALL *(Continued)*

Variations: (1) As participants become more skilled, increase the difficulty of the activity by adding an extra challenge (make a target with different things to aim at for Station #1, have players use nondominant hand to throw, and so forth). (2) Create variations for each station (have participants make their own targets to use for Station #1, for instance, or place a tire between partners for Station #2 and have them attempt to make the ball bounce inside the tire on its way to the other person).

SOFTBALL SKILLS STATIONS

Grades: 4 – 6

Purposes: To provide practice in all softball skills
To improve coordination and dexterity

Equipment: Several softballs and three bats

Description: Divide the players into four groups. Designate an area for each activity, and assign a group to each area. Establish a rotation pattern to be followed by groups when the signal to switch is given.

This activity can be used for one or several physical education periods, or it can be used to begin each softball session prior to the actual game.

Station #1) THROWING/CATCHING: Players get into pairs and stand ten to twenty feet apart, facing each other, leaving plenty of space between themselves and the next pair. Participants take turns throwing and catching, taking a step back after each throw until they are throwing as far as they can while maintaining accuracy and good throwing form.

Station #2) INFIELDING: One person is chosen to throw or hit grounders to the rest of the group. Fielders can take normal positions on an infield, or they can space out in any field area. After each player has had several turns, a new person becomes the batter or thrower until each has had a chance at both activities.

Station #3) OUTFIELDING: One person is chosen to throw or hit flies to the rest of the group. The others spread out an appropriate distance and attempt to catch fly balls. The first one to catch three flies becomes the new batter or thrower, and the batter takes a spot in the outfield.

Station #4) BATTING: One person in the group is chosen to be the batter. One player is assigned to be the pitcher. The rest of the players scatter about the outfield to retrieve the balls that are hit. The batter is given ten pitches, then the pitcher moves to the batter's spot, and one of the fielders comes in to pitch. Each player should be given a chance at all positions.

SOFTBALL SKILLS STATIONS *(Continued)*

Variations: (1) Include an accuracy challenge to the throwing/catching station (hang a tire from the backstop and have players throw at the target, have partners attempt to throw and catch without having to move their feet, and so forth). (2) Have players throw the ball "around the horn" after each grounder is caught on the infielding drill. (3) At the outfielding station, give fielders incentive for catching a ground ball as well. One fly is worth 100 points, and each grounder is worth 25 points. When a fielder gets 300 points, s/he comes up to bat or throw. (4) At the batting station, allow the batter to run the bases on the tenth pitch, and if s/he gets a home run, s/he is allowed ten more pitches.

BUCKET CHUCK IT

Grades: K–3

Purposes: To improve throwing accuracy
To improve catching and fielding skills
To provide practice in base running

Equipment: A small playground ball and a bucket, box, or can for each group

Description: Divide participants into groups of five to ten. For each group, establish a starting line and place a bucket about twenty yards away. One player is chosen to begin as the thrower, and stands behind the starting line. The other members of the group scatter evenly on the playing field.

The object for the thrower is to throw the ball as far as possible between the fielders. As soon as the ball is thrown, the runner runs to the bucket and back to the starting line. The fielders try to retrieve the ball and throw so that it lands in the bucket before the thrower crosses the line. Fielders must throw from where they pick up the ball. The team in the field can make as many attempts as possible before the thrower crosses the line. Players take turns throwing, and the game continues.

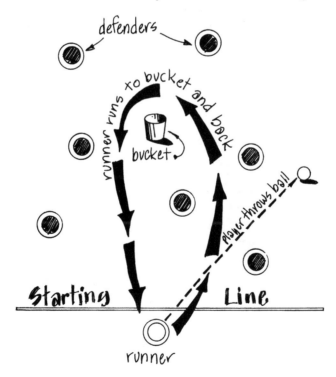

Variations: (1) Change the throwing challenge for the fielders (attempt to make the ball land in the hoop on the ground, knock over the plastic bottle, and so forth). (2) Have two or three people throw and run at the same time. (3) Set up bases that the thrower must step on as if rounding a base path instead of having them run to the bucket and back.

SKEETER

Grades: K–3

Purposes: To develop throwing accuracy
To improve quickness, agility, and coordination
To provide practice in base running

Equipment: A foam rubber ball for each person, and a few hoops, pieces of carpet, or anything that can serve as a base

Description: Divide the participants into groups of five to eight players. Each group needs a few objects that can serve as base markers. Scatter base markers in a circular pattern, several yards apart. Each player needs a foam ball.

One person is chosen to stand in the middle, as the other members in the group form a tight circle around him/her. The person in the middle throws the ball (it helps if the middle person has a ball that is bigger or a different color) as high as s/he can, and all other players throw their balls in an attempt to hit it before it touches the ground. If someone is successful, s/he takes the next turn in the middle. If no one hits the ball, they all scramble toward the bases, while the middle person attempts to tag another player before he/s can reach one of the bases. When tagged, that player switches with the middle person, and the game continues.

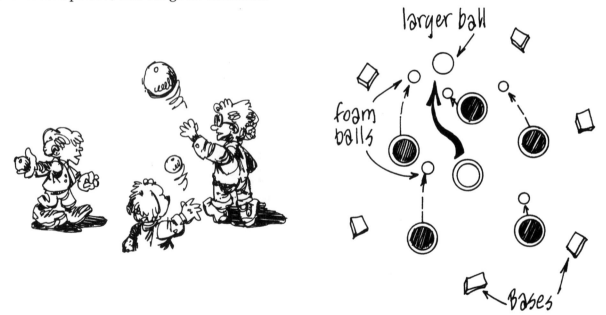

Variations: (1) Change the throwing challenge (all players attempt to throw their ball into a bucket, through a hoop, at an object on the ground, and so forth, before they scramble to the bases. (2) Change the method of locomotion players must use to get to the bases (for instance, hop, skip, roll). (3) To provide practice in base running, have players run in a circular pattern and touch each base instead of just one.

AROUND THE HORN

Grades: K–6

Purposes: To improve softball throwing, catching, fielding, and base running skills

Equipment: A softball and four base markers

Description: Set up the field as in regular softball with three bases and a home plate. Divide the players into two equal teams and have one team form a line behind the backstop. The others assume regular softball positions, except that in addition to the normal infielders, one person stands on each of the bases (the catcher stands behind home plate until the action begins).

The first person stands on home plate and throws the ball anywhere in fair territory and immediately begins to run the bases. A point is scored for each base the runner manages to touch before the defense can throw the ball "around the horn." The object for the defensive team is to retrieve the ball, throw it to the catcher, who then throws to first base, and then the ball must travel the rest of the way "around the horn" to second, third, and finally back to the catcher at home plate.

An out can be recorded each time the ball beats the runner home, and teams could either switch after three outs, or after each member of the batting team takes a turn.

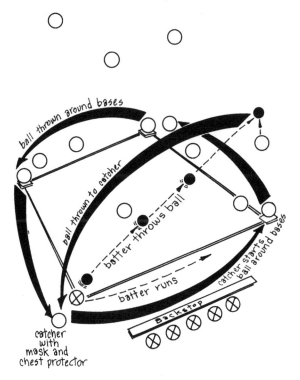

Variations: (1) Play *Double Play* instead, where fielders must retrieve the ball, throw to the shortstop, who flips to second, and the second base player completes the double play by throwing to first. The runners progress is stopped when the double play has been completed. Also, change the location of the double play (third to second, home to third, and so forth). (2) Allow batters to hit instead of throw the ball. (3) Break into smaller groups and have several games going at the same time.

WORK-UPS

Grades: K– 6

Purposes: To improve all softball skills

Equipment: A ball and bat

Description: Players are assigned to all the normal softball positions. Extra infielders and out-fielders can be positioned to allow for more players, and to make hitting more challenging. The remaining players are assigned to a batting order. All regular softball rules apply during the game.

Play begins as those in the batting order attempt to hit. Batters remain in the batting order as long as they continue to hit safely. When a batter makes an out, or forces someone into an out on a fielder's choice situation, s/he takes the field as the new right fielder. Thus, when a batter makes an out, all fielders move up one position in the fielding rotation order. The exception is when a fielder catches a fly ball, in which case the fielder is placed directly into that person's spot in the batting order, and the batter takes the position of the person that caught the fly ball, instead of becoming the right fielder.

The game continues until all players have had a chance to play each position in the field, and have had a turn at bat.

Variations: (1) Play a round in which players must "switch hit." (2) Have batters move to right field after three times at bat to keep the rotation moving quickly. (3) For young players, play the game using a "T-ball" apparatus.

WORK-UPS *(Continued)*

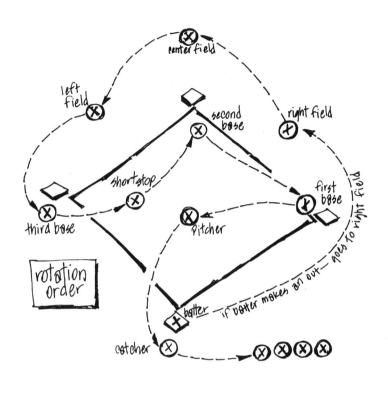

BIG BASE BALL

Grades: 4 – 6

Purposes: To provide practice in softball hitting, fielding, and throwing skills
To promote cooperative play and strategy formation

Equipment: A softball, a bat, two base markers, a home plate marker, and an old sheet, blanket, carpet, cones or anything available to mark off a large base area

Description: Place first, third, and home plate in the regular positions for softball. Mark a *Big Base* area (6' by 6') a bit farther out than second base would normally be. Divide the group into two equal teams, and have one team assume regular softball positions in the field, while the other team lines up behind the backstop.

The first batter begins the action by hitting a ball pitched by a member of the defensive team into fair territory. The object for the batter is to run to the Big Base area before the ball gets there, without being tagged with the ball by an opponent. The runner can choose to stay at the base or run home. Once a runner leaves the base s/he cannot return, except on a caught fly ball. Several people may be in the Big Base area before one or all attempt to score a run by reaching home plate without being tagged with the ball by one of the opponents.

The object for the defense is to field the ball and throw it to the Big Base before the runner arrives. The fielding team can also make an out by catching a fly ball, or by tagging a runner that is attempting to score at home plate.

Batters should be given as many pitches as they need to hit a fair ball. After three outs are made, or when all the members of the offensive team have had a turn to bat, the teams switch and the game continues.

BIG BASE BALL *(Continued)*

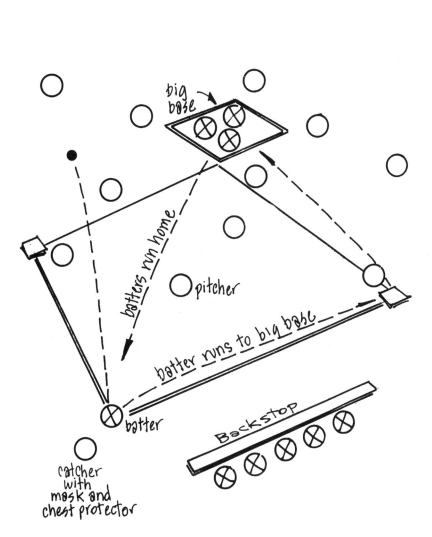

Variations: (1) Play Siamese Big Base Ball where runners must hold hands and attempt to score in pairs. (2) Play a round of *Everything's Fair* where any ball hit is in play. (3) Make it harder for the person trying to score by requiring runners to run backwards, push a partner "wheelbarrow" style, zig-zag through a series of cones, and so forth, as they make their way toward home plate.

SOFTBALL WITH A WIGGLE

Grades: 4 – 6

Purposes: To improve softball hitting, fielding, throwing and base running skills
To increase quickness, agility, and balance

Equipment: Four or more pairs of flags or strips of cloth, a bat, ball, and bases

Description: Set up the field for a regular softball game. Divide the group into two equal teams, and have one team form a line behind the backstop. The first four or all of the batting team should put on flags. The defensive players assume regular softball positions. In addition to the regular fielders, one flag puller is assigned to play between each pair of bases (one between home and first, another between first and second, and so on).

Regular softball rules apply as batters hit the ball into fair territory and run the bases. The difference is that to get a runner out, the defense must pull his/her flag when they are not touching a base. The object for the runner is to work his/her way around the bases without getting a flag pulled. The goal for the defense is to pull the flag from runners before they can score a run at home plate. The defense must field the ball and get it to the pitcher before the flag pullers can challenge the runners.

Flag pullers are not allowed to block the base line, and runners are not to run into flag pullers. Runners are to use twists, fakes, rolls, jumps, or other movements to get by the flag pullers. A caught fly ball is an out, and a flag pulled from a runner not on a base results in an out. After three outs are made, the teams switch places and the game continues.

Variations: (1) Use a playground ball and have the batters hit the ball with their fist. In this version, the flag pullers convert to hitting runners with the ball below the waist. (2) Allow runners to remain on the bases until both flags are pulled. In this version, a player crossing home plate with only one flag scores half a run, and when the defense gets only one flag, half an out is recorded.

SOFTBALL WITH A WIGGLE (Continued)

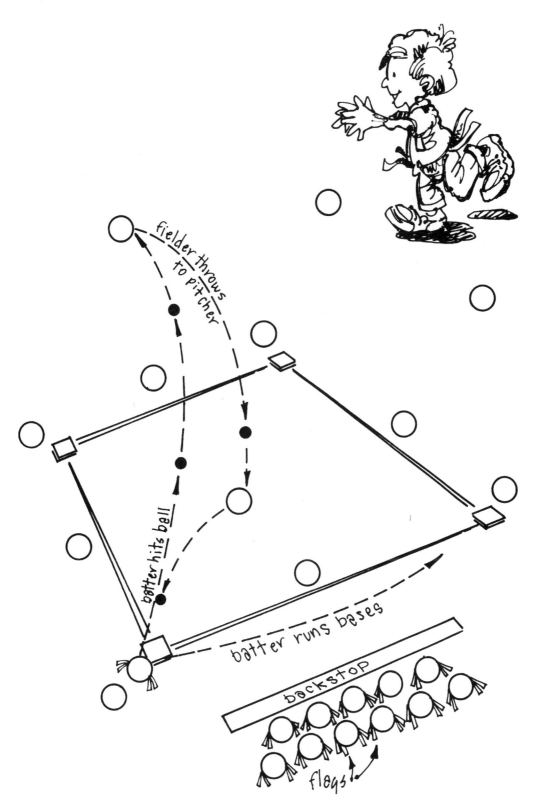

fielder throws to pitcher

batter hits ball

batter runs bases

backstop

flags

BOOMER

Grades: 4 – 6

Purposes: To improve all softball skills
To help children feel successful at hitting

Equipment: A Boomer Bat or an old tennis racket, and a tennis ball or 4" rubber ball

Description: Regular softball rules are used to play the game, but you'll want to have all fielders back up a few steps! The object of the game is for all batters to be able to hit the ball, and hit it farther than they ever have before. All players will feel successful after connecting with the ball using the Boomer Bat. A tennis ball can be used, or use a 4" rubber ball for better sound effects. Back everyone up and "play ball!"

To make a Boomer Bat, you'll need an empty five gallon water jug, and a thick piece of dowelling. The dowel needs to have the same diameter as the neck of the jug. Insert the dowel so that it touches the bottom of the jug, and extends out the top about two feet. Bolt or screw the jug to the dowel at the top of the neck, and put a long screw through the bottom of the jug, extending up into the dowel two to three inches. Tape an old sponge or piece of cloth around the bolt or screws on the neck so that they are not exposed.

Variations: (1) Use a tennis racket instead of a Boomer Bat. (2) Play a game in which batters must "switch hit." (3) Experiment with different balls (1"hard rubber ball, Nerf baseball, and so forth).

OVER THE LINE

Grades: 4 – 6

Purposes: To provide practice in hitting a ball accurately
To improve fielding skills

Equipment: A bat, ball, bases and a batting tee if desired

Description: Divide the group into two equal teams. One team is up to bat first, while the other team covers the field in the positions described below. Use cones, markers, or chalk to mark a twenty foot section beginning at the base path and extending into the outfield.

Three defensive players are allowed to stand inside the twenty foot zone, while the rest spread out beyond the zone to cover the outfield. The batter can hit fungo style, off a batting tee, or use a pitcher from their own team. Offensive players do not run the bases; teams keep track of imaginary runners to tabulate the score.

Each player gets two chances to hit the ball. An out is recorded when any fielder catches a fly ball, or when a batter hits two foul balls or misses the second attempt. A ball that lands in front of the twenty foot zone (a grounder) is considered a foul ball. A single occurs when a ball is hit into fair territory, and is not caught by the fielders before it hits the ground. A home run occurs when a ball is hit over the last outfielder, or the ball passes by all fielders untouched and ends up beyond the last outfielder.

Invisible base runners move up one base each time a single occurs, and a home run clears the bases. Teams can switch after three outs, after five minutes of batting, or after all members of the team have had a chance to bat.

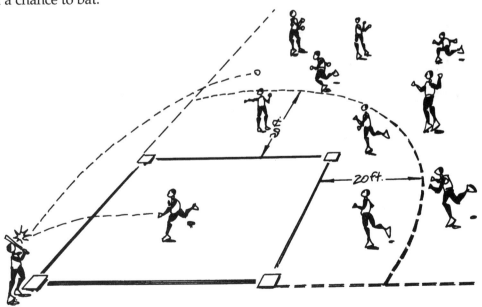

Variations: (1) Add doubles and triples into the scoring system by allowing a double when a ball is touched and dropped by a player inside the twenty foot zone, and allowing a triple for a ball mishandled by an outfielder. (2) Break into smaller groups by playing a three-on-three version of the game. In this situation, close one side of the field and have three defensive players cover the entire area past the line.

SOCCER

Lead-Up Games

SKILL DEVELOPMENT STATIONS FOR SOCCER

Grades: K–3

Purposes: To provide opportunities for primary grade children to develop skills that can later be used in soccer

Equipment: Several soccer balls, some cones, and some balloons

Description: Divide the participants into five equal groups. Assign each group to a different station, and establish a rotation pattern to be followed when the signal to switch is given. Set up the stations so that participants have adequate space for each activity, and in such a way that the leader and helpers can monitor all stations efficiently.

Station #1) DRIBBLING: Set up a course using cones that forces participants to make sharp turns as well as gradual changes in direction. Have them take turns dribbling a soccer ball the entire length of the course.

Station #2) DRIBBLING WITH FEET, THIGHS, AND HEAD: Provide a balloon for each person at the station. Have individuals keep the balloon aloft for as long as possible using kicks with their feet, as well as using their head, chest, and thighs to keep the balloon from hitting the ground.

Station #3) PASSING: Have participants form pairs and stand several feet apart. They take turns kicking the ball back and forth as accurately as possible. The receiving person should trap the ball with one foot to bring it to a stop before kicking it back to his/her partner. When pairs have mastered the skill, they can move farther apart or attempt to kick the ball back and forth without bringing it to a stop.

Station #4) THROW IN: Place a tire or hoop on the ground and have participants form a circle several feet back from the hoop. Players take turns using a two-handed overhead throwing motion as they attempt to make the ball bounce inside the hoop on its way to another person in the group. When participants demonstrate mastery, everyone in the group can take a step backwards, and repeat the activity.

Station #5) LONG DISTANCE KICKS: Set up a pair of cones several feet apart, and have one person stand between the cones as a goalie would. Participants try to kick the ball from several yards away so that it passes through the cones. The goalie can either stand behind the cones and retrieve the ball, or s/he can stand in front of the cones and attempt to stop the ball from passing between the cones. Have participants rotate each time so that they each get a chance to kick and play goalie.

SKILL DEVELOPMENT STATIONS
FOR SOCCER *(Continued)*

Variations: (1) As participants become more skilled, increase the difficulty of the activity by adding an extra challenge (for example, have pairs pass back and forth while running to a cone and back for Station #3, use a foam rubber or soccer ball for Station #2, have participants use their non-dominant foot for Station #5, and so forth). (2) Create variations for each station (play as a group instead of doing Station #2 individually, set up cones in a circle or figure eight for Station #1, and so forth).

SOCCER SKILLS STATIONS

Grades: 4 – 6

Purposes: To provide practice in all soccer skills
To improve foot-eye coordination and agility

Equipment: One soccer ball for each station, and several cones or markers

Description: Divide the players into as many groups as there are stations. Designate an area for each activity, and assign a group to each area. Establish a rotation pattern to be followed by groups when the signal to switch is given.

This activity can be used for one or several entire physical education periods, or it can be used to begin each soccer session prior to the actual game.

Station #1) DRIBBLING: Set up cones in a line, five to ten yards apart, from one side of the field to the other. Players form a line at one side of the field, and the first person in line dribbles the ball in a slalom fashion to the last cone and back. Players should use both feet equally to control the ball as they make their way down and back.

Station #2) PASSING: Have players form two lines, facing the same direction, about ten yards apart. Players dribble and pass, back and forth, to the far end of the field and back.

Station #3) SHOOTING/GOAL TENDING: One person is chosen to be the goalie. This station requires a goal of some kind (regular soccer goal, cones or markers set an appropriate distance apart). The rest of the players form a line twenty to thirty yards from the goal. The object is for the player with the ball to dribble to a distance of about ten yards from the goal and take a shot. The shooter becomes the new goalie, and the goalie moves to the end of the shooting line.

Station #4) HEADING: Players form a circle. One player begins the activity by tossing the ball up and heading it to someone else in the group. The object is to keep the ball aloft as long as possible using only head shots.

Station #5) CORNER KICK: Divide the players into two equal groups. One group forms a line at the corner of the field, while the other group lines up in the center of the field, about ten yards out from the goal. A corner kick is made by the first person in the kicking line, and the field player attempts to score by heading, kicking, or using any legal shot to send the ball through the goal.

Station #6) THROW-INS: Players form two lines, facing each other, five to ten yards apart. Players take turns making legal throw-ins to each other. Participants should take a step back after each turn until they are throwing as far as possible, while maintaining accuracy and legal technique.

SOCCER SKILLS STATIONS *(Continued)*

Variations: (1) Move cones closer together for dribbling station. (2) Add a defender to the passing activity. (3) Add a fullback as a defender in the shooting drill, or make shooters approach from an angle. (4) Allow foot and knee shots at the heading station and have groups keep track of how many times they can touch the ball before it hits the ground. (5) Insert a goalie during the corner kick drill. (6) Have players make throw-ins to their partners down a sideline while others defend.

HOOPLA

Grades: K–3

Purposes: To improve kicking accuracy
To provide practice in defensive skills

Equipment: A hoop, tire, or piece of carpet or paper for each player, and a soccer or playground ball for each group

Description: Divide the participants into groups of five. Four members of the group form a large square, and each player stands inside a hoop. The fifth player stands in the center of the square.

The "Hoopla" begins when one of the players standing in a hoop attempts to kick the ball to another hoop player. The person in the center is free to roam as s/he attempts to steal the ball from the others. The hoop players must make accurate passes to their teammates, who cannot leave their hoop to receive a pass. When the defensive player steals the ball, or when a player must leave his/her hoop to receive a pass, a new person becomes the defender and the action continues.

Variations: (1) Play without a defender until skills develop to the point where one can be included. (2) Increase the number of hoop players in the group and have two defenders. (3) Allow hoop players to move using a one foot in, one foot out of the hoop method. Players can also be allowed to shuffle with both feet inside the hoop. (4) Play *Hula-hoop Hoopla* where players can move about as long as they are "doing the hula."

KICKOUT

Grades: K–3

Purposes: To improve kicking control and accuracy
To improve defensive skills

Equipment: One foam rubber, soccer, or playground ball for each group

Description: Have the players form a large circle with about six feet between each person. Choose one person to stand in the center of the circle. The player in the middle has the ball to begin the game.

The object for the player in the middle is to attempt to kick the ball between the defensive players so that it passes through the circle. The players forming the circle act as goalies, and use feet, body, and hands to try to keep the ball from exiting the circle. When the ball is controlled by one of the goalies, or passes through the circle, a new person moves to the center of the circle and the game continues.

Variations: (1) Break into groups of five to ten and have several games going at the same time. (2) Have two or more players inside the circle. (3) Play a version where goalies must attempt to stop the ball without using their hands. (4) Play a version where no one plays inside the circle. In this version all kicks are made by circle players. (5) Play Circle Kick Tag where one or more people are inside the circle and the object is for circle players to kick the ball so that it hits one of the players inside the circle.

FOOTBAG FRENZY

Grades: K– 6

Purposes: To improve foot-eye coordination
To increase flexibility
To improve soccer skills

Equipment: A Hacky Sack or other type of footbag, or a beanbag, balloon, or wad of paper

Description: Playing with a footbag is a great way to work on foot-eye coordination for both the dominant and nondominant foot. It is also a good activity for creating comradeship in a cooperative situation.

Have the players form groups of two to eight and form a tight circle. Demonstrate the basic footbag kicks, which are the toe kick, the inside kick, and the outside kick. Players may also contact the footbag with their head, knees, or upper torso. The only parts of the body that players are not allowed to use are the hands and arms.

One of the participants begins the action by tossing the footbag to someone else in the group. The object is for each player to control the footbag for one or several kicks and then pass the bag to someone else. The goal is simply to keep the footbag aloft for as long as possible, while attempting to include all members of the group equally.

inside kicks   outside kick   knee kick   toe flick

Variations: (1) A balloon can be used with more success for beginning players. The balloon will provide more time and a greater margin of error for each kick. (2) For more advanced players, a low string can be set up for *Footbag Volleyball*, where volleyball rules apply as players kick and head the ball back and forth over the net. (3) Play *Footbag Foursquare* where players attempt to keep the footbag aloft and avoid having it land on the ground inside their square.

FOUR CORNERS SOCCER

Grades: K– 6

Purposes: To improve all soccer skills

Equipment: One soccer ball

Description: Divide the group into two teams, and have the teams spread out along opposite ends of the playing field. To begin the game, the leader blows a whistle, or calls out, "Corners," and kicks or throws the ball into play. It is best to kick the ball toward the team that is behind, to give them the advantage for that round, and to avoid collisions at the center of the field.

The action begins as players from each of the four corners of the lines run toward the ball. The object is to work as a team to advance the ball toward the opponents' goal and kick the ball across their line. The entire end line is the goal area, and line players have goalie status as they try to prohibit the opposing team from kicking the ball across their line. Line players are allowed to move anywhere along their line, but they cannot move forward into the playing area to stop a goal attempt.

The round is over when a goal is scored (must pass through goalies at head level or below), or when a line player controls the ball after a scoring attempt. When the round is over, the field players go back to the middle of their lines, and the next round starts with the new corner players. All regular soccer rules apply to the action on the field.

Variations: (1) The leader calls out, "Two," or "Three," meaning that two or three players from each corner run out to be field players for the round. (2) Use two balls at the same time. (3) Play a round in which line players can kick the ball back into play until a goal is scored.

FOUR CORNERS SOCCER *(Continued)*

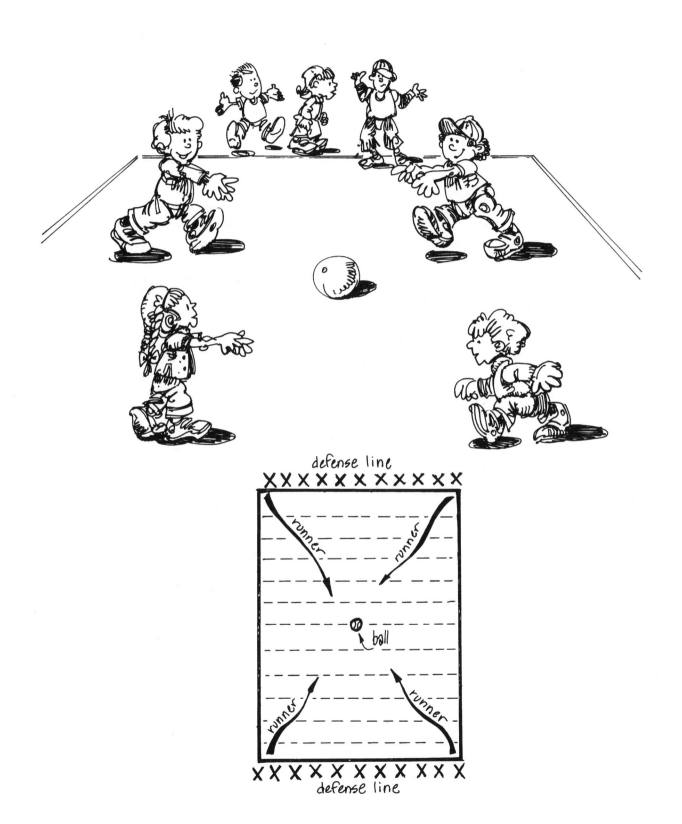

defense line

ball

defense line

SIDE BY SIDE SOCCER

Grades: K– 6

Purposes: To improve all soccer skills
To promote cooperation between players

Equipment: One soccer ball, and enough old bicycle tires, hoops, or pieces of material for every pair of players (if desired)

Description: Divide the group into two teams, and have each player find a partner. In pairs, players assume regular soccer positions. Players need to be connected in some way. They may be holding onto a hoop, old bike tire, or piece of cloth, or they may simply hold hands. Goalies may play individually, or you might want them to play in pairs as well.

Regular soccer rules apply during the game, with the additional challenge of players having to remain connected to each other as they move the ball and attempt to score by kicking the ball into their opponents' goal. When players become disconnected, the result is the same as in any similar soccer violation, which is a free kick by the opposing team from the spot where the infraction occurred.

Variations: (1) If using hoops or tires, have pairs get inside the hoop or tire to play. (2) Play a round in which players form groups of three or four.

ALLEY BALL

Grades: 4 – 6

Purposes: To improve coordination
To increase flexibility
To develop soccer understandings and skills

Equipment: A nine-inch soft rubber ball
Chalk or masking tape to mark the alleys

Description: Teams A and B, playing against each other, try to bat the ball (with a clenched fist) over the other team's end line. Each team has a player in each of the three alleys, and the other players are side or end guards, positioned as shown in the playing field diagram. Players must remain in their own alleys (and between the restraining lines) and guards must remain outside the field. Play begins at center field when the teacher drops the ball. The alley players attempt to move the ball across their opponents' end line (below waist level in order to score) and the guards seek to keep the ball on the field and within the control of their own team players. After the scoring of a point, or a designated time, players 1, 2 and 3 leave the field and take the positions of the highest numbered players on their team. Players 4, 5 and 6 move into the alleys and the other players rotate accordingly. Play resumes when the ball is again dropped at center field.

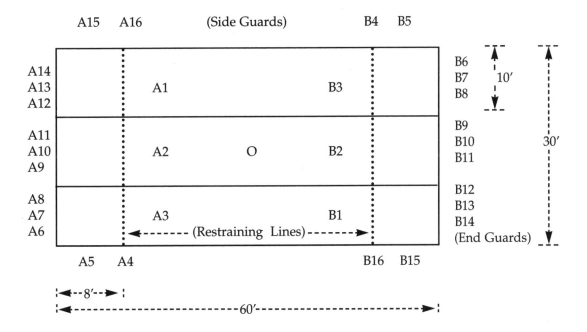

Variations: (1) The game may be played in a multipurpose room or gymnasium. (2) Alley ball can be modified to allow for feet only; in this variation it is recommended that the ball be deflated partially (or use a soft Nerf ball) so that it cannot be kicked farther than the length of the field.

ALLEY BALL *(Continued)*

FOUR-WAY PELE

Grades: 4 – 6

Purposes: To improve all soccer skills
To provide a lot of action for all participants

Equipment: One or more soccer balls and enough cones or markers to make four soccer goals

Description: Divide the group into four equal teams. The field can be set up in a number of ways. A standard rectangular soccer field can be used with goals at both ends, in the normal position, along with an additional goal in the middle of each sideline. When using the format described above, rotate field position each time a goal is scored. Goals can also be set up in the corners of a rectangular field. Another way to arrange the game is to mark off a square field and place goals in the middle of each sideline.

Regular soccer rules apply as teams try to score on any of the three opposing teams while defending their own goal. Each team should assign one goalie and a fullback, with the rest of the players considered halfbacks who can go anywhere on the field. All players can get a lot of action and have a lot of fun in this wild version of soccer!

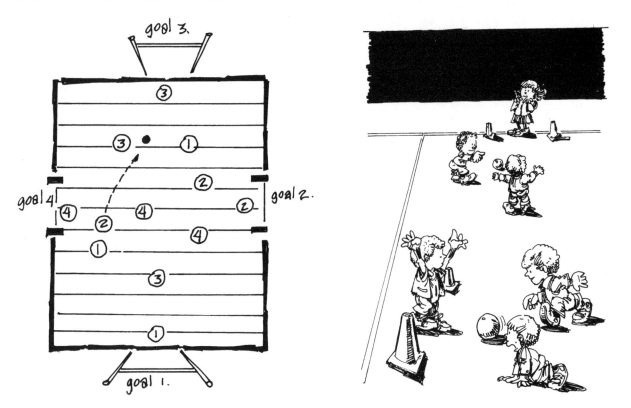

Variations: (1) Use two balls at the same time. (2) Play the game using the *Four Corners Soccer* (*see* Table of Contents) format.

VOLLEYBALL

Lead-Up Games

SKILL DEVELOPMENT STATIONS FOR VOLLEYBALL

Grades: K–3

Purposes: To provide opportunities for primary grade students to develop skills that can later be used in volleyball

Equipment: Several balloons, beachballs, and/or large Nerf balls

Description: Divide the participants into five equal groups. Assign each group to a different station, and establish a rotation pattern to be followed when the signal to switch is given. Set up the stations so that participants have adequate space for each activity, and in such a way that the leader and helpers can monitor all stations efficiently.

Station #1) BUMPING: Have participants use a bumping motion to keep a balloon aloft for as long as they can. Each person should have his/her own balloon.

Station #2) BUMPING: Provide enough balloons so that each person has his/her own. Have participants bump the balloon against a wall, catch it , and repeat the motion. If successful, have them attempt to bump the balloon against the wall continuously, without catching it each time.

Station #3) SETTING: Have players use a setting motion to keep a balloon aloft, with a partner or in small groups.

Station #4) SERVING: Have participants work with a partner and use a serving motion to hit a balloon back and forth. Each person should catch the balloon before serving it to their partner.

Station #5) BUMPING: Have participants work in pairs for this activity. People take turns throwing a balloon to their partner, who tries to bump the balloon as accurately as possible back to the other person, who tries to catch it before it hits the ground. Have participants alternate roles each time.

SKILL DEVELOPMENT STATIONS
FOR VOLLEYBALL *(Continued)*

Variations: (1) As participants become more skilled, have them try more challenging pieces of equipment (beachballs, large foam rubber balls, or volleyballs). (2) Add an extra skill challenge to each activity (try not to move feet at all, use nondominant hand, and so forth). (3) Use variations for each station (for example, lie on back for setting motion, try to makes serves pass through partner's arms).

VOLLEYBALL SKILLS STATIONS

Grades: 4 – 6

Purposes: To provide practice in all fundamental volleyball skills
To improve hand-eye coordination

Equipment: Four volleyballs and one volleyball net

Description: Divide the players into four equal groups. Designate a spacious area for each of the four stations. Assign each of the four groups to a station, and establish a rotation pattern to be followed by groups on the signal to switch.

This activity can be used for one or several entire Physical Education periods, or it can be used to begin each volleyball session prior to an actual game.

Station #1) SETTING: Have players form a circle. Instruct participants to set the ball using an overhand setting technique. They should attempt to keep the ball aloft for as long as possible by setting the ball to someone other than the player next to them. An alternative is to have one of the people in the group face the rest of the group, and to have that person toss the ball to one of the setters, who then sets it back to the person who tossed the ball.

Station #2) BUMPING: Have the players form a circle. Players must bump the ball to a participant other than the one next to them. The object is to keep the ball aloft using controlled and accurate bumps. Once again, an alternative method is to have one member of the group face the rest and toss the ball to a player, who then bumps the ball back to the person who tossed the ball to him/her.

Station #3) BUMPING (PASSING) A SERVE OR SPIKE: Divide players into two groups for this station. The groups form single file lines, facing each other, about ten to twenty feet apart. The first player in the hitting line uses an overhand hitting or serving motion to send the ball toward the first player in the receiving line. The object is for the receiver to bump the ball accurately, as if passing it to a teammate. The bumper retrieves the ball and tosses it back to the next player in the hitting line. Each player rotates to the end of the other line after each attempt, so that all players get practice hitting and receiving.

Station #4) SERVING: Divide the players into two groups. This station requires a court with appropriate boundaries and a net. Half the group forms a line at the serving area on one side of the court, while the other players do the same on the other side. Players take turns attempting serves, and return to the end of their line after each attempt. The front player for the receiving side can step forward and attempt to bump the ball, or you may want them to simply catch it and serve it back.

VOLLEYBALL SKILLS STATIONS *(Continued)*

Variations: (1) Include conditioning stations where participants run or do other activities as part of each rotation. (2) As the players progress, add accuracy challenges for each station (try to get the serve to land in a garbage can placed in the middle of the court, place hoops on the ground and have bumpers attempt to make the ball land inside, and so on).

CONTROL YOURSELF

Grades: K–3

Purposes: To improve bumping and setting skills
To promote control and accuracy
To promote cooperation

Equipment: A balloon, volleyball, or large foam rubber ball for each group, and a carpet sample, piece of paper, or any marker for each player

Description: Have players form groups of four. Place carpet samples or similar markers on the ground so that each group forms a square with players about three feet apart. A standard 4-square court can be used if available. Distribute a balloon or ball to each group.

The object of the game is for the players to use bumping and setting motions to keep the ball aloft in a very controlled fashion. The goal is for players to keep at least one foot on the marker or in their square during the activity. Groups keep working to improve their own record as time allows.

Variations: (1) Have players lie down on their markers and play a round where some part of their body must stay in contact with the marker. (2) Play a relay version where a line of three or four people is formed at each marker. In this version, after a player hits the balloon, s/he quickly runs to the back of the line, while the next person in line steps up to cover the next shot.

BEACHBALL BARRAGE

Grades: K–3

Purposes: To improve all volleyball skills
To provide an aerobic workout
To provide an opportunity for continuous activity by all participants
To have a lot of fun

Equipment: Several beachballs, balloons, or large foam rubber balls, and a volleyball net

Description: Set up a volleyball net at an appropriate height, or substitute with a piece of string or rope tied to chairs or desks. Have participants scatter on both sides of the net evenly.

The leader begins the action by putting one ball in play at a time until several balls are in motion. Players attempt to keep all balls aloft and send them back and forth over the net. This is meant to be a wild and fun activity, therefore rules and proper technique are not stressed. (For example, players should simply pick up a ball from the ground and immediately put it back into play; more than three hits might be used on a particular ball to send it back over the net, and so forth.) Once all the balls are activated, the game runs continuously for as long as time allows.

Variations: (1) Use several modified nets (string tied to chairs) and have several games with small groups going at the same time. (2) After all balls have been activated, work back down to one ball by eliminating any ball that touches the ground. (3) Have all players lie on their backs for a round.

ONE BOUNCE VOLLEYBALL

Grades: K–6

Purposes: To improve all volleyball skills
To simplify the game, which allows beginning players a chance to practice all volleyball skills

Equipment: One volleyball

Description: Divide the group into two teams, and have them establish positions on opposite sides of the court. Regular volleyball rules apply during the game, except that the ball must hit the ground once before a player hits it each time it passes over the net. After the first hit, players have the option of hitting the remaining two shots in the air, or they can let the ball bounce once after each player hits it. The ball must be returned to the opposing team on the third hit, or sooner, as in regular volleyball.

Once players get used to letting the ball bounce once each time it passes over the net, the game becomes easier and it is more likely that a rally will occur. This allows beginning players to practice all volleyball skills to a greater extent than when playing regular volleyball.

Variations: (1) Allow the ball to bounce as many times as necessary to keep the ball in play. (2) Allow the receiving team to catch the ball after a serve. Have a player bump, set, or toss the ball to another player for a set, and a third player hit the ball over the net. This version promotes an even more controlled game, allowing for more practice on bumping, setting, and hitting skills.

VOLLEYBACK

Grades: K– 6

Purposes: To improve hand speed and quickness, and hand-eye and foot-eye coordination
To introduce or reinforce volleyball skills
To have lots of fun

Equipment: One or several beachballs or large foam rubber balls, and a net or piece of rope

Description: This game is played on grass with a volleyball net or piece of rope suspended at a very low height (2'– 4'). Mark boundaries large enough for all participants to fit inside, but small enough so that there is minimal open space. Divide the group into two equal teams and have participants scatter about on their side of the court, and lie down on their backs.

The leader gives the beachball to a different person each time, and that player serves the ball over the net to begin each rally. The object is to bat the ball from player to player until it can be hit back over the net, while not allowing the ball to hit the ground. Teams are allowed as many contacts as they need to get the ball back over the net.

Regular volleyball scoring can be kept by awarding a point or side-out each time the ball contacts the ground. For a cooperative rather than competitive game, teams can work together to see how many times they can successfully hit the ball over the net without letting it touch the ground on either side.

Variations: (1) Use at least two, or several balls at the same time. (2) Have a few players from each team help keep the ball in play by allowing them to stand up along the sides of the court and bat the ball back to teammates rather than letting it go out of play. (3) Play a round where participants kneel instead of lie on their backs. (4) Have players use their feet instead of their hands.

"TIRED FEET" SERVING PRACTICE

Grades: 4 – 6

Purposes: To improve serving consistency and accuracy
To increase balance and catching skills
To promote quickness, agility, and cooperation

Equipment: A volleyball and several old bike tires or hoops

Description: Have several players assume receiving positions on one side of the net, each standing inside an old bike tire or hoop. One person is chosen to serve the ball first, and stands behind the end line on the opposite side of the net.

   The object for the server is to serve the ball in bounds to a spot where the receivers will be unable to catch the ball. The goal for the receivers is to catch a designated number of serves, before the ball touches the ground, without moving their feet outside of their hoop. Once a person has caught the designated number of serves, s/he changes places with the server and the game continues.

"TIRED FEET" SERVING PRACTICE *(Continued)*

Variations: (1) Play a version where several players are in line to serve. Each person serves once. If the ball is caught, they change places with the person that caught it. If the ball is not caught, the server takes a spot at the end of the serving line and moves forward to serve again as play continues. (2) Add a task to the game to increase the challenge. For example, have the server run to the center of the court and bump an additional ball ten times in a row without letting it touch the ground, while the receivers shuffle around the perimeter of their side of the court, keeping their feet inside the hoops. If the server accomplishes the task before the receivers finish theirs, the caught serve does not count. (3) Place the tires on the ground, and have the receivers act as shaggers. The server must make the ball land inside a tire. If successful, s/he keeps serving. If not, the server must run around the outside of the court before the receiving team can throw the ball from person to person until each has been included. If the receiving team wins the race, a new server is chosen.

ACE BALL

Grades: 4 – 6

Purposes: To improve jumping and catching skills
To introduce or reinforce volleyball skills
To promote teamwork and cooperation

Equipment: A volleyball and a net or piece of rope

Description: This game is played on a standard volleyball court, with a net or piece of rope suspended at the usual height. Divide the group into two equal teams, and have the players assume regular volleyball positions.

Ace Ball is played like regular volleyball, with a few exceptions. The object is to win the point or get a side-out on each rally, but the larger goal is to "Ace" opponents. An "Ace" occurs when the defensive team is unable to touch the ball before it hits the ground after it passes over the net from the opponents' side. Regular volleyball scoring is kept while playing the game to eleven or fifteen, however, an "Ace" is worth two points to the team that served the ball, or one point and a side-out for the team that received the serve.

In Ace Ball, players can use regular volleyball bumps, sets, and spikes. They are also permitted to catch the ball and throw it to a teammate or over the net, as long as they are in the air when they catch the ball and release it before they touch the ground. Once the players get the hang of Ace Ball, some interesting moves and strategies will develop!

ACE BALL *(Continued)*

Variations: (1) Play *Task Ace Ball*, where in addition to a double point for an "Ace," the team that got "Aced" must run a lap around the court, do ten push-ups, and so forth. (2) Play *Elimination Ace*, where each time an "Ace" occurs, the team that got "Aced" must send one of their players to the other team. Play until one team is eliminated totally. (3) Have a *Slam Dunk Ace Exhibition*, where groups of three do a combination of three moves, including one player receiving a serve and throwing it to a setter, who then throws it to one of the teammates, who finishes the play off with a "power slam" over the net. This game is just for show, thus no defensive team is required. (4) Make the court huge, so that teams have to cover a lot of ground. (5) If more nets are available, break into smaller groups and have several games going at the same time.

FOUR-WAY VOLLEYBALL

Grades: 4 – 6

Purposes: To improve all volleyball skills
To get more players involved in a volleyball game

Equipment: One volleyball, two volleyball nets, or two lengths of rope suspended at normal net height

Description: Divide the players into four teams. Use cones to form a large enough area to accommodate the number of players in the game. Set up two volleyball nets, intersecting at right angles at the center of the court, to make four equal zones.

Play begins as one team serves the ball to any of the other three courts, and regular volleyball rules apply during Four-way Volleyball. If the serving team wins the point, they retain the serve. If a side-out occurs, the serve rotates to the next team in a clockwise pattern. All four teams compete against each other in this game, thus allowing more participation for larger groups of players.

Variations: (1) Use two balls at the same time. (2) Give the serve to the team that last touched the ball when a point is scored. (3) Use the *One Bounce Volleyball* (*see* Table of Contents) rules while playing this game.

FLAG FOOTBALL

Lead-Up Games

SKILL DEVELOPMENT STATIONS FOR FOOTBALL

Grades: K–3

Purposes: To provide opportunities for primary grade children to develop skills that can later be used in football

Equipment: Several Nerf footballs, some cones, a few sets of flags, and a kicking tee

Description: Divide the participants into five equal groups. Assign each group to a different station, and establish a rotation pattern to be followed when the signal to switch is given. Set up the stations so that participants have adequate space for each activity, and in such a way that the leader and helpers can monitor all stations efficiently.

Station #1) PASSING AND CATCHING: Have participants work in pairs to practice throwing and catching skills by standing a few feet apart and taking turns throwing and catching a Nerf football. When pairs demonstrate throwing accuracy and catching consistency, they can each step backwards to continue.

Station #2) RUNNING: Use cones to set up a course that forces participants to make gradual as well as sharp changes in direction as they run with the football while eluding imaginary defenders.

Station #3) DEFENSE: Have a set of flags for each person at the station. One person is the defensive player attempting to pull his/her partner's flag as s/he attempts to run from one cone to another several yards away. They then switch roles and repeat the activity.

Station #4) KICKING: Place a set of cones several feet apart and have participants attempt to punt or place kick a Nerf football so that it passes between the cones.

Station #5) RUNNING AND CHASING: Mark boundaries for a small circle with cones. One person holds a football and attempts to avoid being tagged by the other members of the group while staying inside the boundaries. Participants take turns being the person holding the football.

SKILL DEVELOPMENT STATIONS
FOR FOOTBALL *(Continued)*

Variations: (1) As participants become more skilled, increase the difficulty of the activity by adding an extra challenge (have receiving partner run a few steps so that passer must lead receiver at Station #1, place objects that participants must jump over as they make their way through Station #2, and so forth). (2) Create variations for each station (have one person chasing all others to pull their flag instead of others chasing the person with the ball at Station #5, play as a group with all members of the group trying to pull the runner's flag at station #3, and so on).

FOOTBALL SKILLS STATIONS

Grades: 4 – 6

Purposes: To provide practice in all football skills
To improve agility, quickness, and coordination

Equipment: Several footballs, some cones, and a kicking tee

Description: Divide the players into four groups. Designate an area for each activity, and assign a group to each area. Establish a rotation pattern to be followed by groups when the signal to switch is given.

This activity can be used for one or several entire physical education periods, or can be used to begin each football session prior to the actual game.

Station #1) PASSING/CATCHING: Players form two groups and get into two lines, facing each other, five to ten yards apart. Participants take turns throwing and catching. After each throw, the passer should take a step back, until partners are throwing as far as they can while maintaining control, accuracy, and technique.

Station #2) RUNNING/DEFENDING: Place two cones about twenty yards apart. One player is chosen to be the defender and stands between the cones. The rest of the people form a line about ten yards from the defender. The object is for the runner to use speed, quickness, and fakes to run past the defender, while remaining inside the boundaries of the cones. The object for the defender is to touch or pull the flag of the runner within five yards in front of, to five yards behind the cones. The runner becomes the new defender, and the defender goes to the end of the line.

Station #3) PUNTING/PLACE KICKING: Have players form two groups and stand twenty to thirty yards apart. The first person in one line steps forward to receive the punt. The person in the other line punts the ball as accurately as possible to the receiver. The receiver punts the ball back to the next person in the opposing line. Players should alternate between punting and place kicking on each turn.

Station #4) CATCHING/PASSING: One person is chosen to be the passer, while the others form a line to the side. The first person in line runs downfield about ten yards, then cuts to the middle of the field on a slant pattern. At this time, the passer releases the ball. The receiver becomes the next passer, and the passer goes to the end of the line.

FOOTBALL SKILLS STATIONS *(Continued)*

Variations: (1) Add an accuracy task to the Passing/Catching drill (receiver tries not to move feet while still catching pass, passer tries to throw the ball through a tire or hoop held up by receiver, and so forth). (2) Have a series of defenders, spaced ten yards apart, for the Running/Defending activity. (3) For the Punting/Place Kicking station, have punters aim for a hoop on the ground or punt angle shots toward the sidelines, and have place kickers attempt to kick through goal posts or have a pair of players form a goal post by joining hands and holding up their outside arm. (4) For the Catching/Passing drill, have receivers run different patterns, or have a defender cover them.

HOOP SCOOT

Grades: K–3

Purposes: To provide practice in football dodging skills
To improve football defensive skills
To improve football passing skills

Equipment: Several bike tires, hoops, or markers

Description: Place several hoops or markers of any kind several feet apart in a large open area. All players except one begin the game standing inside one of the hoops. There can never be more than three players inside one hoop at a time. One player is chosen to start the game as the chaser.

The action begins when the leader blows a whistle, and the object is for players to run from one hoop to another without getting tagged by the chaser. People are not allowed to remain in a hoop for more than five seconds. The leader can help facilitate this rule by blowing a whistle every five seconds. The game goes on continuously as players use speed, quickness, and agility to keep from being tagged. When someone is tagged by the chaser, the two switch roles and the game continues.

Variations: (1) Have two or more chasers at the same time. (2) To work on throwing accuracy, play *Hoop Keep Away*, where people must pass the ball and make catches without stepping outside their hoops. If a pass is dropped or a player misses the ball, or if the chaser intercepts the ball, a new chaser takes over, and the game continues.

THROW THE PIGSKIN AND GRIN

Grades: K–3

Purposes: To improve football passing skills
To provide practice on defensive skills
To improve football dodging skills

Equipment: Cones or markers of some kind, and a football

Description: Have players form groups of five to ten. Use cones or markers to establish boundaries for a large open area. Players spread out inside the boundary markers, and one person is chosen to be the first chaser.

The object is for players to keep the ball away from the chaser, and to avoid being tagged while holding the ball. Players may run with the ball or catch it and throw it to someone else immediately. The chaser attempts to intercept the ball or tag someone that is holding the ball. When the chaser is successful, a new chaser is chosen, and the game continues.

Variations: (1) Play a version where each person that gets tagged becomes a chaser until only one player is left. (2) Play *Catch and Run* where one person throws the ball as high as possible and all players attempt to catch it. The person that catches the ball attempts to run to the boundary line without being tagged by another player.

FLAG WAG

Grades: K– 6

Purposes: To improve running and dodging skills for football
To improve football defensive skills

Equipment: Two football flags, pieces of material, or strips of paper for each player (if desired)

Description: The game can be played on a football or soccer field, or cones can be used to mark end lines and sidelines in any open space. All players need to be equipped with a pair of football flags, or they may simply tuck pieces of cloth or strips of paper (folded over several times for strength) into their pockets or waistband.

Two players are chosen to begin the game as flag pullers. They position themselves at least ten yards back from the starting line. All remaining players form a line along the end of the playing field. The game begins when the leader blows a whistle, and the object is for the runners to make it to the other end of the field without getting their flag pulled.

When a player does get her flag pulled, s/he becomes a flag puller at the beginning of the next round. The game continues until only one to five players are left as runners. The remaining players become the new flag pullers, and a new game begins.

Variations: (1) Play a round in which players don't become pullers until both flags are pulled. (2) If flags aren't available, play the game by having defensive players tag other players with one hand.

ONE HUNDRED (100)

Grades: K–6

Purposes: To practice football throwing and catching skills
To practice "mental math"

Equipment: A football

Description: The game can be played on a softball diamond, or on any open field area. One person is chosen to be the passer, and in the softball field version, stands behind home plate with the football. If not on a diamond, the passer simply takes a position at one end of the play area. The rest of the participants spread out, giving each other plenty of room, at a distance that they estimate to be the limit of the passer's potential.

The passer throws the ball to different sections of the field, trying not to allow fielders to anticipate the direction of the pass. Players in the field attempt to catch the passes before the ball touches the ground. The object is for fielders to be the first one to accumulate 100 points. A ball caught before it touches the ground is worth twenty points. A ball fielded cleanly after it hits the ground, but before it comes to a stop on the ground, counts as five points. When a player reaches 100 points s/he switches with the passer, and the game continues.

Variations: (1) Have players punt or place kick the ball rather than throw it. (2) Have two or more passers at the same time. (3) Once the players understand the game, form smaller groups and have several games going at the same time. (4) Put a garbage can near the place where the passer stands, and let fielders attempt to throw the ball back so that it lands in the can for an extra ten points. (4) Make the "mental match" part of the game more challenging by changing the value of the catches and make the winning points total 2-3/4, 10.5, and so forth.

VOOTBALL

Grades: K–6

Purposes: To improve football throwing and catching skills
To promote teamwork and cooperation
To help participants become more familiar with volleyball rules and scoring

Equipment: A regular or Nerf football and a volleyball net or piece of rope

Description: The game can be played on a grass, indoor, or blacktop volleyball court. A regulation net can be used, or a piece of rope can be substituted if a net is not available. The net should be high enough so that even the tallest player has to throw the ball using an upward arch to clear the net. Divide the group into two equal teams, and have them take positions on opposite sides of the court as in regular volleyball.

The object of the game is to pass the ball over the net so that it hits the ground on the opponents, side of the court. The players on the defensive team use quickness, agility, speed, and sure hands to cover as much of the court as possible when receiving the ball.

One team begins the action by having one player stand behind the service line and throw the ball over the net so that it lands inside the other team's side of the court. Each team can use up to three contacts on each possession. For instance, a back row player might receive the serve, pass the ball to a front row player on the left side, who then might pass to a front row player on the other side, who then must pass the ball back over the net. A point or side-out occurs when one team manages to throw the ball so that it hits the ground directly, or is dropped by a player from the other team. As in regular volleyball, a point can only be scored by the serving team, otherwise, when the ball hits the ground it is a side-out and possession changes. Players rotate as in volleyball when they gain possession on a side-out, so that all participants get a chance to play every position.

Speed should be encouraged in this game by implementing a one-second rule. The leader should explain to players that a side-out or point will result when a player holds on to the ball for more than one second at any time.

VOOTBALL *(Continued)*

Variations: (1) Play the game on a football field and use the goal posts instead of a net. (2) Play an "up in the air" version of Vootball where players must jump up, catch the ball, and throw it to a teammate or back over the net before they touch the ground. (3) Play a round where two points are scored for a ball that hits the ground without being touched, and one point is scored for a dropped ball.

FOUR DOWN SIDEWAYS FOOTBALL

Grades: 4 – 6

Purposes: To improve all football skills
To provide a format where all participants are involved in each play

Equipment: A football for each group, and some cones or markers to set up the fields

Description: Form groups of three to six players per team. Assign two teams to each field. Use cones or markers to lay out the number of fields needed. If markings for a full-sized football field already exist, simply play Sideways Football by making the sidelines represent the end zone lines, and use ten-yard markings as sidelines. If no lines exist, mark off several fields approximately twenty yards by forty yards.

Teams on offense are allowed only four downs to move the ball toward the end zone and score. Only pass plays are allowed, and all players on the offensive team are eligible to receive passes, with one person playing quarterback. Each person on the defensive team covers one of the receivers, with the exception of one person who is chosen to rush the quarterback.

Flags may be used, or two hand touch rules can be implemented as the way to stop an offensive player's progress. A three or five second delay count can be used by the defensive player rushing the quarterback to allow pass patterns to develop. A team can choose to go for a touchdown or punt on the fourth down. If a fourth down attempt is unsuccessful, the defensive team takes over possession on the previous line of scrimmage.

goal line

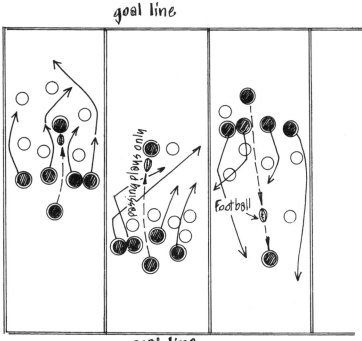

goal line

FOUR DOWN SIDEWAYS FOOTBALL *(Continued)*

Variations: (1) Have players rotate one position each play so that all players get the chance to play each position. (2) Include after points and field goals in the game by having defensive players hold hands to form a goalpost and crossbar, with the outside people raising their outside arm straight up to serve as the uprights. (3) Allow the quarterback to run the ball if a receiver isn't open.

THROW AND GO

Grades: 4 – 6

Purposes: To improve football passing and catching skills
To improve defensive pass coverage skills
To provide a fast-action game in which all players participate continuously

Equipment: One football

Description: The game can be played on a football field, or cones can be used to mark boundaries for a large rectangle in any open area. If there are no existing lines, use cones to establish a midline across the width of the field. Divide the group into two teams, with teams spread out on their half of the field, covering their area as evenly as possible.

To start the game, the leader throws the ball to a player (once the game is under way, the leader should throw the ball to the team that is behind to give them the advantage), and as soon as the receiver controls the ball the action begins. The object is for a team to use a combination of quick passes, along with running and dodging, to advance the ball across the opponents' goal line.

After receiving a pass, a player can advance the ball until s/he is tagged by a defensive player. When a player is tagged, s/he must stop running, and throw the ball to a teammate within five seconds. A player may throw the ball to a teammate on the run, before being tagged. There is no blocking allowed in this game, players should instead be instructed to spread out to make themselves available for a pass, which will also help them to be in position to cover the field defensively should a turnover occur. When the ball, or a player, goes out of bounds, the team in possession enters the ball with a pass from the point where it went out of bounds.

A turnover occurs when the defensive team intercepts a pass, or when the ball hits the ground because of an errant pass or a deflection. The action does not stop when a change of possession occurs. After the ball hits the ground or is intercepted, the new offensive team attempts to advance the ball toward their opponents' goal immediately. Play does not stop until one team successfully crosses their opponents' goal line with a completed pass in the end zone, or when a player runs across the goal line before being tagged.

After a point is scored in this nonstop action game, have teams reset themselves on opposite sides of the field, toss the ball to a player from the team that is behind, and let the fun continue!

Variations: (1) Use different pieces of equipment to play the game (Frisbee, tennis ball, Nerf football, and so forth). (2) Use the *Four Corners Soccer* (*see* Table of Contents) format, where small groups of players from corners of lines along the end zone engage in competition.

THROW AND GO *(Continued)*

scoring
line

middle
line

scoring
line

● team 1.
○ team 2.

KICKBALL VARIATIONS

Lead-Up Games

ONE-THREE-FIVE STAY ALIVE

Grades: K–6

Purposes: To improve kicking and fielding skills
To promote teamwork and cooperation between fielders

Equipment: A rubber or Nerf kickball and some cones

Description: To set up the field, place a home base and three cones in line with each other. One cone should be near the pitcher's mound, another where second base would be, and the third out in center field. Use a few cones to mark off a safety zone (roughly twenty feet in diameter) around home base.

Divide the group into two teams. One team is at bat, and the other team scatters about the field to cover the entire area, as there is no such thing as a foul ball in this game.

The game begins with the pitcher rolling the ball toward the first kicker. S/he kicks the ball in any direction, and runs toward the cones. The kicker must decide which cone to run around before returning to home base. The object for the fielding team is to retrieve the ball and hit the runner (below the waist) before s/he can round a cone and get safely back to home base. Catching a fly ball does not count as an out. To promote teamwork in the field, a player can only take three steps after gaining control of the ball, then s/he must pass it to another player, forming a relay system to move the ball closer to the runner. To make the game more challenging, fielders cannot throw at a runner from inside the safety zone.

A successful trip around the first cone and back scores one point, around the second and back is a three-point score, and around the farthest cone and back to home base safely is worth five points. When the fielding team has hit three players before they arrive at home base safely, the teams switch positions and the game continues.

ONE-THREE-FIVE STAY ALIVE *(Continued)*

Variations: (1) Rather than having the fielding team hit opponents with the ball, have them throw the ball to a catcher at home base to make an out. (2) Allow players to make as many trips around the cones as they can before being hit. For example, a player may make a three-point trip, and still have time to make another one-point trip.

TEAMWORK KICKBALL

Grades: K– 6

Purposes: To improve kickball and other skills using a format that allows for more participation than regular kickball

   To promote teamwork and cooperation

Equipment: A kickball and four base markers

Description: The game is played on a regular kickball field with three bases and a home plate. Divide the group into two equal teams, and have one team assume regular kickball fielding positions, while the other team forms a line behind the backstop. One person from the defensive team rolls the ball toward home plate, and the first kicker for the offense kicks the ball into fair territory to begin the action.

   The object for the runner is to touch as many bases as possible before the defensive team can complete their task. One point is scored for each base touched before the defense finishes. To stop the runner's progress, or record an out, the defensive team must throw the ball to each member of the team. An out is recorded when the defense manages to get the ball to each team member before the runner crosses home plate. A caught fly ball is not an out. The defensive players are not allowed to move once the ball has been fielded; they must make throws and catches from the position they were in when the ball was caught originally. After three outs are made, the teams switch positions and the game continues.

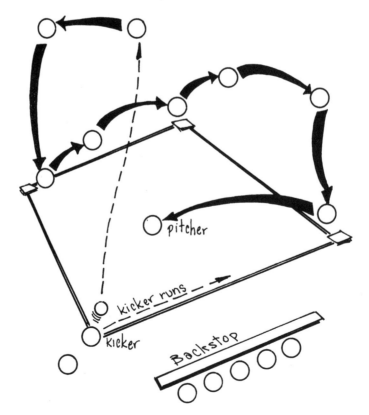

TEAMWORK KICKBALL *(Continued)*

Variations: (1) Change the task to be completed by the defense (all team members must pass through a bike tire, players kick the ball to each other instead of throwing the ball, the team forms a line and they must "hike" the ball to each other, and so forth). (2) Have offensive players throw a football, Frisbee, or tennis ball instead of kicking the ball.

KICKBALL-BASKETBALL

Grades: K– 6

Purposes: To reinforce kickball and basketball skills
To improve kicking, catching, passing, and shooting skills
To promote teamwork and cooperation

Equipment: A kickball, three cones or markers, and a home plate marker

Description: This game is played on a basketball court, and if possible, use a court that is bordered by grass. Place home plate at one corner of the court (next to grass if available). Place three cones, in a line, about ten yards apart, outside the court in either direction. Divide the group into two equal teams, and have one team scatter about the basketball court and the surrounding area, while the other team forms a line well away from home plate, on the opposite side from where the cones are placed.

One person from the defensive team is chosen to be the pitcher, and one person from the offensive team stands behind home plate. The pitcher rolls the ball toward home plate, and the kicker kicks the ball anywhere in fair territory (the sideline and end line of the court extend out indefinitely). The object for the kicker is to run to one of the cones and back to home plate before the other team can shoot a basket. The nearest cone is worth one point, the middle one three points, and the farthest cone counts as five points. The defensive team uses basketball passes as they attempt to move the ball toward the hoop and get it to one of the team members close enough to shoot the ball into the basket before the runner crosses home plate. If they manage to make a shot before the runner reaches home, an out is recorded. A caught fly ball is not an out. After three outs are made, the teams switch places and the game continues.

KICKBALL-BASKETBALL (Continued)

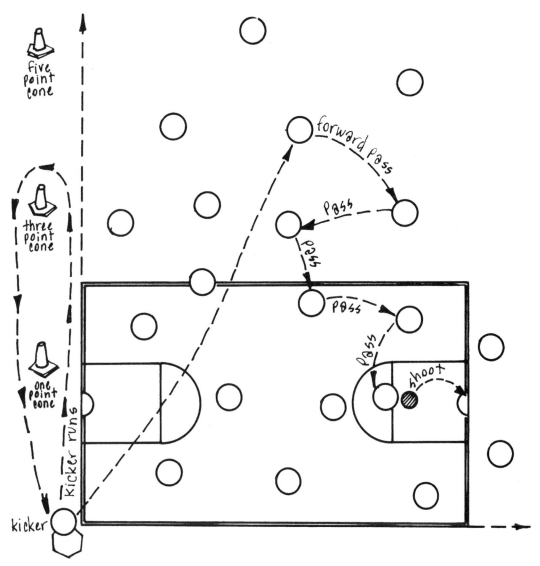

Variations: (1) Play *Kickball-Basketball-Soccer,* where the runner must dribble a soccer ball down and back instead of simply running. (2) Extend the cones farther out and have the defensive team make a pass to each member of the team before they can take a shot at the basket.

THREE-BALL DO IT ALL

Grades: 4 – 6

Purposes: To improve all kickball skills
To promote cooperation and teamwork between fielders
To provide fielders with more opportunities to participate
To help kickers feel successful

Equipment: Three balls that can be kicked

Description: Put a piece of masking tape on each of the three balls. On one ball, write #1 on the tape, on the second ball mark #2, and on the third ball write #3. Set up the field as you would for a regular kickball game. Divide the group into two teams, with one team at bat and the other team scattered about the entire field, because there is no such thing as a foul ball in this game.

The game begins with the first kicker placing all three balls on the ground at home base. S/he kicks each ball in any direction as fast as possible, and runs toward first base. One point is scored for each base touched before the fielding team accomplishes its task. The object for the fielding team is to relay the ball marked #1 to first base, the one marked #2 to second base, and the ball marked #3 to third base. When all three balls are controlled by players standing on the bases, the runner can score no more points. Thus, a kicker can score 0, 1, 2, 3, or 4 points per turn. There are no outs in this game, therefore, each player on the kicking team takes a turn, and then the teams switch places and play resumes.

THREE-BALL DO IT ALL *(Continued)*

Variations: (1) Allow players to continue running around the bases until the fielding team has the balls in place (thus, a kicker could score 5, 6, 7, 8, or more points per turn). (2) Allow players to pick up the balls and punt them rather than kick them from the ground. (3) After fielders successfully control the balls and the runner is eliminated, have them roll the balls toward home base, and if a ball touches the base, the fielding team subtracts one point per ball from their opponents' score.

KICKBALL, AND A WHOLE LOT MORE

Grades: 4 – 6

Purposes: To practice kickball skills
   To provide an opportunity for introducing conditioning and skill challenges as part of the fun game

Equipment: A kickball and whatever materials needed for the tasks assigned at bases

Description: Set up the field with three bases and a home plate as in regular kickball. Explain and demonstrate the tasks to be completed at each of the three bases. Divide the group into two equal teams, and have one team take the field in regular kickball positions, while the other team forms a line behind the backstop. The defensive team chooses one player to pitch, and the offensive team sends the first kicker to home plate.

The pitcher rolls the ball toward home plate, and the kicker kicks the ball into fair territory, and runs toward first base. The object for the kicker is to touch and complete the required activity for each base, and cross home plate before the ball arrives. The defensive team must retrieve the ball, throw it to each base, and finally get the ball to the catcher at home plate before the runner gets there. The person at each base for the defense must also complete the designated activity before throwing the ball to the next base. A point is scored each time a runner reaches home plate before the ball does. An out is recorded each time the defensive team manages to get the ball to home before the runner can complete all the tasks and touch home plate. A caught fly ball is not an out.

The activities at the bases can be conditioning movements. Examples would include challenges such as having participants jump rope ten times without a mistake, complete ten push-ups using good form, or jump over a box twenty times without stopping. Skill challenges can also be set up at bases. Examples in this case would include activities such as dribbling a soccer ball to a cone and back, dribbling a basketball to the nearest court and making a basket, batting a balloon in the air twenty times without letting it touch the ground, throwing a tennis ball so that it comes to a stop inside a tire that is placed ten feet away, and so forth. The possibilities are endless for fun and challenging activities at the bases, so set up some good ones and play Kickball, and a Whole Lot More!

Variations: (1) Have the players suggest and set up different base activities. (2) Have the base activities set up so that it takes two or three people working together to complete the tasks. In this version, one of the offensive players kicks the ball and teammates join in to travel around the bases with the kicker.

KICKBALL, AND A WHOLE LOT MORE

(Continued)

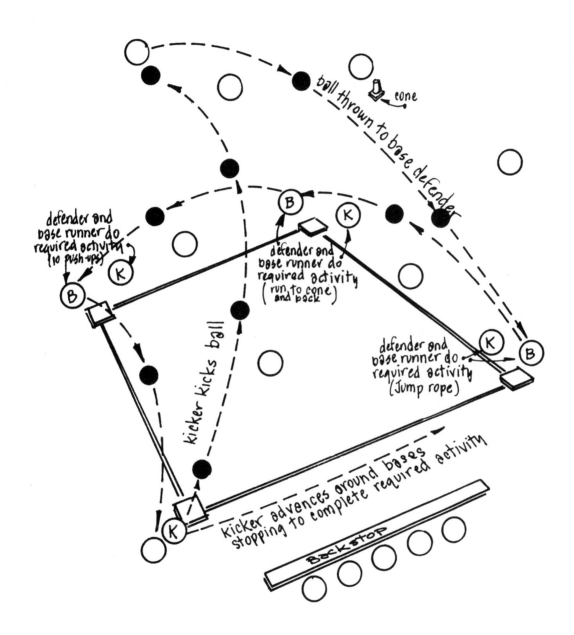

ball thrown to base defender

cone

defender and base runner do required activity (10 push-ups)

defender and base runner do required activity (run to cone and back)

defender and base runner do required activity (jump rope)

kicker kicks ball

kicker advances around bases stopping to complete required activity

Backstop

SUPER HOOPER

Grades: 4 – 6

Purposes: To provide practice in kicking, catching, and throwing
To promote cooperation and formation of strategies
To include more people in the action of the game

Equipment: A kickball and a few hoops or old bike tires

Description: Divide the group into two equal teams, with one team up to kick and the other team scattered evenly in the field. Do not allow any defensive players closer to home plate than where the pitcher stands. Place three to six hoops or tires in a semicircle just outside of where a normal base path would be. Place two to four additional hoops approximately twenty feet to each side of home plate, in foul territory.

The kicking team chooses one person to be the pitcher. The kicker kicks the ball anywhere into fair territory, and based on the location of the ball, makes a decision on where to run. On a short kick, the runner may choose to go to one of the hoops on the side, in which case s/he can run to one of the hoops in the field on a teammate's kick. On a long or well-placed kick the runner can run directly to one of the hoops in the field, but must wait until a teammate's kick to return. A point is scored each time a person makes it to a hoop in the field and back to home plate safely. On any given kick, 0, 1, or several runs can be scored. Only one person is allowed in each hoop at a time, so when they are all occupied, someone must attempt to score on the next kick.

The defensive team attempts to field the ball and hit any runners (below the waist) that are outside of the hoops with the ball. A caught fly ball is not an out. More than one out can be recorded on a given kick. Teams can change places after a certain number of outs, after a certain number of minutes, or after all team members have had a chance to kick.

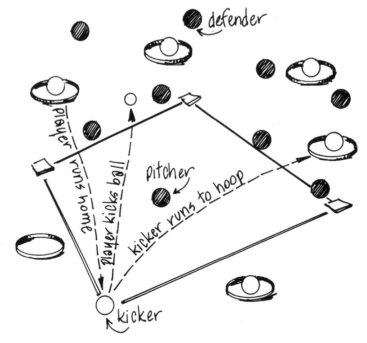

SUPER HOOPER *(Continued)*

Variations: (1) Place the hoops different distances from home plate and assign various point totals for each one. (2) To promote more teamwork, don't allow defensive players to take any steps while holding the ball. Players must use a relay method to move the ball toward the runner. (3) Use two or three balls for a crazy version of this game. The game can move as fast as the pitcher can retrieve the balls and pitch them to new kickers. (4) Play a *"No Fouls"* version where hoops are placed in a full circle and every kick is considered a fair ball.

IV SOMETHING A LITTLE DIFFERENT

*Students will enjoy the ten SOMETHING A LITTLE DIFFERENT activities
that include creative equipment and specialized skills.*

VIDEO HIGHLIGHT DELIGHT

Grades: K– 6

Purposes: To build individual self-esteem and group camaraderie
To practice skills in all areas of physical fitness
To have lots of fun during and after the activity

Equipment: A video camera and whatever participants choose to use

Description: Everyone likes to be the star of the show! This activity gives everyone a chance to "do their thing" for the camera. Allow individuals or groups an opportunity to warm up and practice doing their best movement, stunt, or activity (jump rope tricks, juggling, acrobatics, dances, and so forth). When groups or individuals appear to be ready, begin roaming with the video camera rolling and encourage people to do their best job for the highlight film. People not being filmed can continue to practice their activity or watch and cheer for those being filmed. Having music playing in the background can add to the production, or a soundtrack can be added later. Introductions and commentary by performers can also be encouraged.

The activity can be used for one or several class sessions, or it can be done periodically throughout the year. When the filming is completed, show the video to the group and enjoy the activity all over again!

VIDEO HIGHLIGHT DELIGHT *(Continued)*

Variations: (1) Play a game of *Video Hide-and-Seek.* In this game, the camera person roams around the playing field trying to catch people in the camera's eye. The object for the participants is to run, dodge, roll, dive, and so forth, to avoid being caught on film. Once again, show the video after the activity for lots of fun and laughs. (2) Use the video as a class film project. Add commentary and other features to the production and show it at Back to School Night or Open House events.

TURN 'EM ALL LOOSE
DUCK DUCK GOOSE

Grades: K–6

Purposes: To provide a format where all participants have a chance to be involved
To improve running, chasing, and dodging skills
To promote teamwork and cooperation

Equipment: Some cones or markers of any kind

Description: Divide the group into two equal teams, and have one group form an inner circle and sit down, while the other group forms a circle outside of them and remains standing. Use cones to mark a large circular perimeter boundary several yards outside of the outer circle of players.

To begin the game, the outside circle team forms a huddle away from the other players. They decide upon a key person to be tapped by their captain, or a certain number of players they will tap before giving the "Goose" signal. The team returns and forms a circle outside of the other team, and they begin to walk around, tapping people on the head in unison, chanting, "Duck, Duck, Duck." When they arrive at the key person or number, they all say, "Goose!" and all members of the outer team run, while the inside people get up and chase the opponents.

The object for the runners is to get across the perimeter boundary line before being tagged. The chasers attempt to catch and tag the person that tapped them on the head. One point is recorded for each person that makes it across the line safely. The teams then switch positions and the game continues.

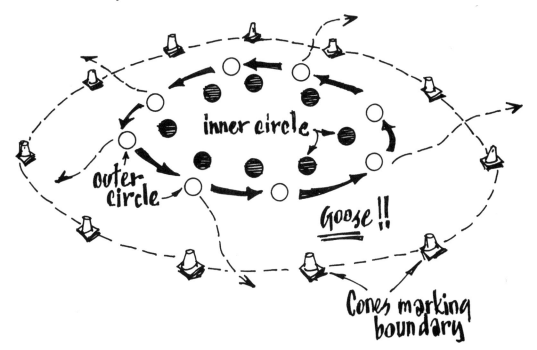

TURN 'EM ALL LOOSE
DUCK DUCK GOOSE *(Continued)*

Variations: (1) Play *Reverse Goose* where the inner circle chants and calls, "Goose!" to begin the chase. (2) Allow taggers to go after anyone from the other team instead of just the person that tapped their head. (3) Change the method of locomotion to be used by both teams (runners have to roll while taggers crab walk, runners must hop while chasers have to run backwards, and so forth). (4) Both teams must accomplish a group task instead of using the run and chase format (for instance, outside team must kick a soccer ball from person to person, while inside team must form a row and backset a volleyball one person at a time until all have had a turn).

FUN WITH JUGS

Grades: K– 6

Purposes: To increase hand-eye coordination
To improve throwing and catching skills

Equipment: A one gallon plastic jug with the bottom cut out for each player, and a tennis ball, Nerf ball, or stuffed nylon ball for each pair of players

Description: Several games can be played using "Fun Jugs" as flingers and catchers. For the first session, let participants get used to the equipment by throwing and catching from various distances until they become adept and accurate at both skills. When it appears that people have become fairly proficient at using the jugs, several new activities can be introduced.

JUG SOFTBALL: Regular softball rules apply as batters must fling the ball with their jug, while fielders must retrieve the ball and throw to bases using only the jug, never touching the ball with their hands.

JUG THROW AND GO: Regular Throw and Go (*see* Table of Contents) rules apply, but players must throw and catch with their jugs. When the ball is on the ground, players must use a scooping motion to retrieve the ball, so that the ball is never touched by the hands.

JUG TAG: One person begins with the jug and a Nerf or stuffed nylon ball. The object is for the person with the jug and ball to chase someone until they are close enough to fling the ball and hit another player with the ball below the waist. The person that gets hit takes the jug and ball and the game continues.

JUG THREE FLIES UP: Have players form groups of four to eight. One person is chosen to be the flinger, while the others scatter about an area at the limit of the throwing ability of the flinger. The fielders attempt to be the first to catch three flies, using a jug to catch the ball. The person that catches three flies first becomes the new flinger.

Variations: (1) Try a game of *Jug Volleyball,* or *Jug Basketball.* (2) When players become very adept with the jugs, set up several accuracy stations (fling the ball so that it passes through a suspended tire, make the ball land in a garbage can, and so forth).

FUN WITH JUGS *(Continued)*

softball

volleyball

tag

Three flies up

TARGET PRACTICE

Grades: K–6

Purposes: To improve throwing strength and accuracy
To promote cooperation and teamwork

Equipment: Several empty boxes, plastic beverage containers, or any lightweight objects, and a tennis or red rubber ball for each player

Description: Divide the group into two equal teams, and have teams stand an appropriate distance apart, depending on grade level, facing each other. If marked lines are not available, use cones, tape, chalk, or rope to mark the lines from which players throw, which are also the goal lines they must defend. Place the targets a few feet apart across the entire play area so that everyone has something to throw, making sure that they are an equal distance from each team.

The object is for each team to move the target items across their opponents' goal line by hitting the objects with the balls. The leader should make sure that opponents are far enough apart to avoid a player being hit by a throw from a player on the opposite side. Also, the leader should caution players to keep their throws low so that the balls roll to the opponents' side of the playing area. Each team needs to assign one shagger to retrieve balls that come to a stop inside the throwing lines, or you can have players wait until the end of the round to gather balls. The leader can stop the action each time a point is scored and reset the targets so that everyone can be involved at all times. Another way would be to allow players to move along the throwing lines and play until all targets have been moved across the goal lines for a point.

Variations: (1) Give each team a "big bopper" ball that can move the targets for a score in one direct hit. (2) Play a soccer round where players kick the balls rather than throw them. (3) Move the lines closer and have players throw with their nondominant hand.

FRISBEE STATIONS

Grades: K– 6

Purposes: To improve Frisbee throwing and catching skills
To increase hand-eye coordination
To promote cooperation

Equipment: A Frisbee for each pair of participants, and some tires, hoops, and any objects that can serve as targets

Description: Divide the players into four groups. Designate an area for each activity, and assign a group to each area. Establish a rotation pattern to be followed by groups when the signal to rotate is given.

Station #1) THROWING/CATCHING: Have the players form pairs, and instruct them to stand ten to twenty feet apart, facing each other. Partners should throw back and forth until both people are tossing with good accuracy, and then both should take a few steps back to increase their throwing distance. Participants should be encouraged to try various throwing techniques other than the standard backhand toss (forehand toss, skip-toss, nondominant hand toss, and so forth).

Station #2) THREE FLIES UP: This activity provides a way to have lots of fun while players practice long distance throwing and catching skills. One person is chosen to be the thrower, and the rest of the group scatters about at a distance they feel is close to the thrower's maximum distance toss range. The object is to catch the Frisbee before it touches the ground three times, at which time the person that caught three flies changes places with the thrower. If a player pushes another person, or interferes with another player's attempt to catch the Frisbee, the offender receives a one fly penalty.

Station #3) FRISBEE KEEP AWAY: This activity serves as good practice for throwing accuracy and catching skills. Players can either form a circle or scatter about within the designated boundaries. One or several people can be chosen to be chasers. The rest of the players attempt to throw and catch the Frisbee in random order, without holding the Frisbee for more than one second, while the chaser attempts to intercept or knock down one of the throws. If the chaser successfully intercepts or knocks down a throw, the person that threw the Frisbee and the chaser switch positions, and the game continues.

Station #4) TARGET SHOOT: This activity helps players work on throwing accuracy. Place one or several tires or hoops on the ground several feet from where attempts will be made. Depending on the availability of equipment, any number of targets can be substituted (cones, balls, boxes, and so on). Allow players to make several attempts at hitting the target, while their partner retrieves the Frisbee and returns it to the thrower.

FRISBEE STATIONS *(Continued)*

throwing-catching

three flies up

frisbee keep away

target shoot

Variations: (1) Set up the stations as a fitness course and have participants engage in each activity for a period of time, and then on the signal to switch, to run to the next station to begin again immediately. You might also want to include additional tasks before players can begin each activity (jump rope 25 times, 10 sit-ups, dribble a basketball 40 times, and so forth). (2) Incorporate different stations into the activity such as *Up in the Air, On the Line,* and *Knock it Down* (*see* Table of Contents). Also, use some of your own ideas, or try suggestions that participants mention.

UP IN THE AIR, ON THE LINE, KNOCK IT DOWN FRISBEE

Grades: K– 6

Purposes: To improve hand-eye coordination
To increase Frisbee throwing accuracy
To have a great time

Equipment: A Frisbee for each pair of players, and a can, milk carton, or similar object for each pair

Description: This activity works best on a paved surface, but it can be played on grass as well. Participants get into pairs and stand about ten to twenty yards apart, facing each other. Pairs need to make sure they have plenty of space between themselves and the other participants. One of the players places the object to be hit an equal distance from where each player will be throwing. Participants take turns throwing the Frisbee, and the object is to be the first one to hit the object in the middle. Score can be kept by awarding one point per hit and two points for a knock down until someone reaches a predetermined point total, or until time expires. Players can also play without keeping score if they prefer.

on the line

knock it down

up in the air

UP IN THE AIR, ON THE LINE, KNOCK IT DOWN FRISBEE *(Continued)*

Variations: (1) Play a round of *On the Line,* where players pick any line on the blacktop to stand on. Each player attempts to throw the Frisbee in such a way that it comes to a stop on the line where the opponent is standing. (2) Play *Up in the Air,* where players must jump before they catch the Frisbee, and release their throw before their feet touch the ground again. This game can be played in pairs, or a circle can be formed and several can play.

FOUR-WAY DISC DELIGHT

Grades: K– 6

Purposes: To improve Frisbee throwing accuracy
To promote teamwork and cooperation
To provide an opportunity for continuous participation for all players

Equipment: Several Frisbees and several playground balls

Description: This game can be played on any surface, but asphalt works best. Use existing lines or mark boundaries for a square or rectangle about twenty yards by twenty yards. Divide the group into four equal teams, and have them line up along the four sidelines of the play area. Distribute Frisbees to several or all participants of two of the teams that are across from each other. Give playground balls to several or all of the players from the other two teams.

One person from each team should be chosen to retrieve the discs and balls that come to a stop inside the play area. Most of the discs and balls will end up at the cooperating team's side of the field, but some will come to a stop in the field. Equipment can either be retrieved after each set of throws, or the action can be continuous, in which case retrievers should wear a catcher's chest protector and mask for safety.

On the signal to begin, the people with the playground balls roll them toward the team across the field. The object is for the people with the Frisbees to throw at the moving targets and hit as many as they can before the balls reach the sideline. Score can be kept in various ways. A point can be awarded to individuals each time they hit a moving ball, or team totals can be kept by totaling point scores for each round until the period ends. The game can get pretty wild and fun, and participants may forget all about keeping score!

The leader can establish a time limit or a certain number of throws for each team if play is continuous. Then teams rotate in a clockwise fashion, so that all teams get an equal number of turns at throwing discs and balls.

Variations: (1) Play a round where the people throwing the balls toss them high in the air instead of rolling them. (2) Break into groups of four so that there is only one player on each sideline. (3) Have one or more small or specially marked balls that count double if hit.

FOUR-WAY DISC DELIGHT *(Continued)*

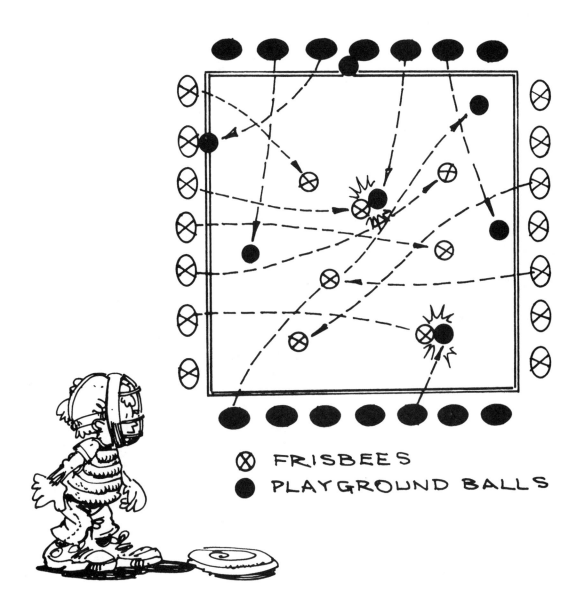

⊗ FRISBEES

● PLAYGROUND BALLS

IT'S HAMMER TIME

Grades: 4 – 6

Purposes: Serves as a lead-up activity for the hammer throw in track and field
To promote teamwork and cooperation
To incorporate a new and different piece of equipment into the P.E. program

Equipment: An old basketball, kickball, Nerf or regular soccer ball with a hole drilled in both sides and a rope fed through and tied off to form a loop

Description: Divide the group into two equal teams. Set up three bases and a home plate as in softball. One team takes the field in defensive positions similar to those used in softball, and the other team is up and forms a line behind the backstop or well out of the way of the thrower.

The first person in line stands near home plate with the hammer throw apparatus. Gripping the rope with both hands, the thrower spins once or twice to generate some power, and lets the hammer fly. You may want to let participants simply fling the hammer with a one-handed underhand fling. If the hammer toss is in fair territory, the thrower runs the bases while the defensive team begins the put-out process. A caught fly ball or force out at a base does not result in an out. To stop a runner's progress, the team in the field must fling the hammer to a person at each base, from first to second to third and to home plate. Once the ball is controlled by the player at home plate, the runner's progress is stopped. Runners get one point for each base touched, and may go around the bases two or more times if it is possible.

You may want to let all the players from the offensive team bat and then have teams switch positions. Another way to play is to record an out when a player does not beat the hammer to home plate, and switch every three outs. In this version, a safe trip around the bases counts as one point.

IT'S HAMMER TIME *(Continued)*

Variations: (1) Play a round where each player on the defensive team must catch and fling the hammer to a teammate to stop the runner's progress, rather than having it thrown to the bases. (2) Play a game where there is no such thing as a foul ball. In this version the defensive team must cover the entire area, and the thrower can fling the hammer in any direction before running.

JUGGLING IS CATCHING

Grades: 4 – 6

Purposes: To improve hand-eye coordination and quickness
To improve the ability to use the nondominant hand
To increase the ability to concentrate
To promote cooperation

Equipment: Several scarves, balloons, bean bags, tennis balls, and various playground balls

Description: Juggling is a great skill to work on from time to time because of the many physical and mental abilities it helps people develop. Not only does it involve numerous athletic skills, it also teaches concentration and serves as a great stress release for people of all ages.

Learning to juggle can be simplified by breaking the process down into individual skills, which can be mastered and eventually put together to produce successful juggling. In addition, techniques can be used to slow down the process, which can be very helpful to beginning jugglers.

The best equipment for learning to juggle is a set of lightweight scarves, and if scarves are not available, balloons are a good substitute. Any objects that stay aloft longer than tennis balls are helpful because they provide much needed time for beginning jugglers. Using lightweight equipment can help reduce the frustration that can occur when learning to juggle.

The best way to learn is to practice and master the individual skills required, and eventually combine those skills to produce successful juggling. The cascade method is the easiest to learn. It is simply tossing an object and making room for it to land by tossing another object. This means there is one ball in each hand and one ball in the air. As the airborne ball starts to drop, the second ball is tossed, making room for the first ball to land. As the second ball starts to drop, the third ball is tossed, freeing up space for the second to land, and so on.

The first step in learning the cascade pattern is to hold one object in the right hand. Toss it to the left hand. Toss it back to the right hand. Repeat the process until throws and catches are consistent.

The second step is to have an object in each hand, and begin by tossing #1 from the right hand to the left hand. As it starts to drop, make room for it to land by tossing #2 to the right hand. Do the same thing starting with the left hand. Repeat the process both ways until throws and catches are consistent.

For step three, begin with #1 and #3 in the right hand and #2 in the left hand. Toss #1 (the toss always begins with the hand that holds two objects). As #1 starts to drop, make room for it to land by tossing #2. As #2 begins its descent, toss #3, catching #3 in the left hand. Repeat the process starting with the two objects in the left hand. Practice until throws and catches from both starting points are mastered.

The fourth step is to add a fourth toss to the previous step. From this point, each progressive step is adding another toss, until the juggler can repeat the process continuously without dropping objects.

This is a great opportunity to allow students to become the teachers as the more skilled participants can help those that are stuck at certain steps. Spending a few minutes each day practicing will allow for a lot of progress, while making sure frustration levels don't rise as participants learn the art of juggling!

JUGGLING IS CATCHING *(Continued)*

Variations: (1) Form a *Group Juggling* station for those that become discouraged or frustrated. Have players form a circle with four to eight people. One person begins by tossing an object to another person (anyone but the person right beside them). The process is repeated until the ball arrives back in the hands of the original person, and thus a pattern is established. Once the group passes the object through the pattern a few times, a second object is added, and it chases the original object through the pattern, and the fun begins! A third object can be added, and then a fourth, and so on. This juggling activity takes a lot of concentration, good communication, and teamwork. (2) Get a local juggler to put on a demonstration at a school assembly to inspire beginning jugglers! (3) Encourage the more skilled participants to develop trick throws and different patterns, and to share them with the others.

CREATE A GAME

Grades: 4 – 6

Purposes: To provide an opportunity for participants to be creative in a cooperative setting
To serve as a catalyst for a cross-curricular unit of study
To generate several new P.E. games

Equipment: Miscellaneous P.E. equipment and various objects found in the classroom

Description: This is an excellent activity that can be developed into a meaningful cross-curricular unit of study. First, have students form groups of four to six members. Round up several pieces of P.E. equipment as well as various classroom objects that seem useful. Give each group three to five objects to use. An example would be to give one group a balloon, a cone, a yardstick, and a chalkboard eraser. Another group might be given a soccer ball, a base, a tennis racket, and an old blanket. Distribute various objects to each group, and explain that each item must be used in their activity.

Allow groups one P.E. period to experiment and implement different ideas using their equipment, with the goal being to invent a new game for others to enjoy. Students should also be given time to produce a written description of their game, including illustrations. Each member of the group should take an active roll in the formation of the game, as well as writing, illustrating, and presenting it to the others.

Dedicate one P.E. period to each group when they are ready to share their ideas. Have the presenters explain the game, using verbal instructions as well as diagrams on the chalkboard, and answer any questions from others before going out to play. The presenters should demonstrate their game outside before actual play begins.

This activity allows participants to showcase their creative abilities as part of a very enjoyable and diverse cross-curricular activity. It provides a format which can incorporate writing, art, oral presentations, reports on games from other cultures, and working in cooperative groups into a physical education unit, while generating several new games for the group to enjoy throughout the year.

CREATE A GAME *(Continued)*

Variations: (1) Once they are familiar with the activity, allow groups to choose three to five objects from a collection of equipment and create more games. (2) Have groups add a piece of equipment to an existing game to give it a new twist! (3) Have students research games from other cultures and present one for the group to enjoy.

V SOME REAL A's

Students get a sense of shared purpose and team effort as they compete in the eight wild relays in this section.

I'M TIRED

Grades: K– 6

Purposes: To improve hand-eye coordination
To increase upper body strength
To improve agility
To have fun while getting exercise

Equipment: An old bicycle tire for each team of four to ten players

RELAYS

(1) Fling Thing: Have teams form lines with players five to twenty feet apart, with teams at least ten feet apart. At the signal to begin, the first person for each team flings the tire to the second person, and so on, until the tire travels down and back several times.

(2) Traveling Fling Thing: Begin with the same format used in #1, but establish a marker to be reached for this traveling version of the tire relay. In this version, as soon as a player flings the tire to the next person in line, s/he runs to the other end of the line. Thus, the tire can keep traveling indefinitely. Have teams relay the tire down and back to a certain marker, or set up a cross-country course.

(3) Can Your Dog Do Any Tricks?: Have players work in teams of three, as they make their way to a marker and back by having two players hold the tire, while the third crawls or jumps through the tire as they make progress. Players rotate roles each time one member of the group passes through the tire.

(4) Swivel Hips: Have teams line up, and place the tires several yards away. Players run down to the tire, step inside, bring it up to their waist, do ten hula-hoop movements, and return.

(5) Tire Task: Have teams line up, and place the tires several yards away. Assign a task to be accomplished by players once they arrive at the tire. For example, players might be required to throw the tire so that it lands around a cone, or participants might have to throw a ball until they can get it to land inside the tire, before returning to their team.

(6) Togetherness Trek: Have players form pairs within their teams, and have pairs run down to a marker and back with both people inside the tire, or grasping the tire with one hand each.

(7) Island Hopping: Have teams line up, and establish a marker several yards away. In this variation, participants can only step inside the tire to make progress. Thus, a person must toss the tire a short distance away, jump and land with both feet inside the tire, lift the tire up and over their head, and repeat the process all the way down and back. This can be done individually, or for an extra challenge, in pairs!

(8) Contortionists Unite!: Have teams form circles and join hands, with two players from each team joining hands inside the tire. At the signal to begin, players move the tire around the circle by passing through it, without letting go of each other's hands at any time.

(9) Who Knows?: Have each team come up with a tire relay idea of their own, and try each one!

I'M TIRED *(Continued)*

WHAT A DRAG

Grades: K– 6

Purposes: To promote cooperation
To provide fun, vigorous exercise

Equipment: An old blanket or sheet for every four to six players

RELAYS

(1) *What a Drag!:* Have groups of four to six players take hold of a blanket which is placed on the ground. One member of the group lies down on the blanket. Teams must drag their cargo down to a marker and back. The relay ends when each person has had the chance to drag, and be dragged!

(2) *Fling-a-ding-thing:* Establish a marker several yards from the starting point. Each team needs a blanket and a ball for this relay. The object is for players to work together to fling the ball as far as possible, run to the ball, pick it up and place it back on the blanket, and repeat the process until they travel to the marker and back.

(3) *Catch 22:* Have four members of each team holding a blanket at waist height. The remaining member of the team stands several yards away, holding any kind of ball. The object is for the player with the ball to throw it to his/her team so that it can be caught using the blanket. When a thrower is successful, s/he runs down to take a turn holding the blanket, while another member of the team runs to the starting point to become the new thrower. The process is repeated until all have had a chance at both tasks, or when one team reaches 22!

(4) *Sheet Skipping:* Have players form pairs within their teams. Pairs roll up the blanket, and each takes hold of one end. The object is to use a traveling jump-rope method (players run forward while working together to hop over the blanket each time it approaches their feet) to get to a marker and back.

(5) *Traveling Low Hurdles:* Have players form groups of three within their teams. Have two people roll up the blanket and take hold of one end, and hold the blanket horizontally about a foot from the ground. At the signal to begin, the third player from each group does a standing long jump over the blanket. As soon as the jumper lands, the blanket holders reset in front of the jumpers, and the process is repeated until the teams of three go to a marker and back. The leader should caution participants to be careful not to trip their teammates. Make sure everyone gets a chance to perform each task.

(6) *The Sky is the Limit!:* Participants will come up with their own variations for new blanket games, so let the players demonstrate their ideas, and continue the fun!

WHAT A DRAG *(Continued)*

SPECIAL APPARATUS RELAYS

Grades: K–6

Purposes: To provide opportunities for various physical challenges
To promote cooperation
To provide entertainment, excitement, and fun

Equipment: Whatever is needed for the relays chosen

RELAYS

(1) *Change of Clothes:* Bring some old clothes and have participants put on pants, shirt, and hat, then run to a cone and back. When one person finishes, s/he takes off the clothes while the next person puts them on, and the race continues.

(2) *Fish Out of Water:* Bring a snorkel, mask and fins, and have participants run with the equipment on while moving arms in a freestyle, butterfly, or breast stroke swimming motion to a cone and back.

(3) *Human Caterpillar:* Use two or more scooters and have people lock legs around the next person's waist. The groups must use their hands to push down and around a cone and back. Another option with scooters is to have one person sit on the scooter while the partner pushes through a race course.

(4) *Rubbish Rage:* Gather a bunch of rubbish (wads of paper, milk cartons, rags, and so forth) and have participants sweep, kick, or carry all the items to a cone and back.

(5) *Snowshoe Race:* Get a pair of paper plates, carpet samples, or lids for each team and have participants slide their feet, keeping them on the items, to a cone and back or through a cross-country course.

(6) *Balloon Blast:* Have participants bat a balloon with their hand to a cone and back or through an obstacle course. Also, have them use different body parts or go in pairs.

(7) *Jug Fun:* Have relay teams form a line and throw and catch with plastic jugs down and back several times. Have participants run down and throw a ball, using a plastic jug, at a target until they hit it, then scoop up the ball and return it to the next person in line.

(8) *Frisbee Frenzy:* Have groups form different shapes (for example, circle, square, rectangle, line) and have them toss the Frisbee to each person to see who can complete the task first. Another idea is to have individuals run to a hoop while balancing a Frisbee on the tip of their finger, toss the Frisbee so that it lands inside the hoop, and return.

(9) *Barrel of Fun:* Pad a fifty gallon barrel and have one person inside while a partner rolls the barrel down and around a cone and back.

(10) *Take Care of the Earth:* Have teams roll an earthball through an obstacle course to see which team can complete the task the fastest.

SPECIAL APPARATUS RELAYS *(Continued)*

change of clothes

fish out of water

human caterpillar

rubbish rage

snowshoe race

balloon blast

Jug Fun

SPECIAL APPARATUS RELAYS *(Continued)*

COOPERATIVE GROUP RELAYS

Grades: K– 6

Purposes: To promote cooperation and teamwork
To introduce or reinforce various skills

Equipment: Whatever is needed for the activities selected

RELAYS

(1) *Traveling Group Relays:* Teams form a line with several feet between each person. A task (for instance, throwing a ball or Frisbee, or kicking a soccer ball) is performed, and the person immediately runs to the other end of the line. The activity continues until the group reaches a marker at the other end of the playing field. Another idea is to have groups form circles with one member inside. The group travels while the person inside performs a task (dribbling a ball, hopping, batting a balloon, and so forth) while remaining inside the circle.

(2) *Out of Body Experience:* Groups form a human chain while seated on the grass. Each person takes a turn being passed the entire length of the chain by his/her teammates.

(3) *Team Leap Frog:* Groups form a line with several feet between each person. All participants assume a bent-knees-hands-on-knees position facing toward the finish line. The last person in line leapfrogs over each member of the team until s/he becomes the first person in line, and then the new last person begins, and so on, until the team reaches the marker. Also, try the same format, but have participants crawl between teammates' legs rather than leapfrog.

(4) *Circle Task Races:* Have relay team members form circles and race to see which team can complete a task first (toss the ball around the circle ten times, kick the soccer ball five times, balance a broomstick or ruler on a finger and walk it to next person twice around the circle, and so forth).

(5) *Multiple Team Relays:* Have four or more teams facing a central location. Teams race to complete a task first. One example would be to have a box full of balls in the center. Each person runs to the box, gets a ball, and dribbles back. The next person dribbles down, puts the ball back, and so on. Another challenge might be to use jump ropes and have one set of turners in the center, facing out, and the other turner the first person in line. Teams race to see which can be first to have all team members jump rope three times in a row before touching the hand of the next person. Jumpers can also attempt to jump each team's rope once and make it back to their team.

(6) *Incredible Edible Relays:* Have teams work together to finish eating a plate of grapes, popcorn, or other tasty treats before the other teams are done. Each person must run down, chew and swallow, then run back. Add to the challenge by having people put on a bib before they eat, and remove it before they return!

COOPERATIVE GROUP RELAYS *(Continued)*

LET'S GET TOGETHER

Grades: K–6

Purposes: To promote togetherness and cohesiveness
To have fun together

Equipment: Whatever is required for the activities selected

RELAYS

(1) *Squeeze It:* Use a balloon or foam rubber ball to connect pairs as they make their way to a marker and back. Examples of activities include events such as *Back-to-Back, Forehead-to-Forehead, Shoulder-to-Shoulder,* and *Hip-to-Hip* relays. If a pair should drop the ball, they must stop and replace it before they continue.

(2) *Balloon Pop:* Have a container full of balloons ready and have teams line up several yards away. Pairs run down, place a balloon between them, and hug and squeeze until they manage to pop the balloon, then run back.

(3) *We're in This Together:* Strap pairs together at the leg and have them travel through an obstacle course where they have to crawl, climb, roll, and so forth, in order to make it back to the next pair.

(4) *Cling-on Relays:* Create a simple or challenging task for teams to attempt as they hook together one at a time during these relays. The first person might run to a marker and back dribbling a soccer ball. Then the second person holds hands with the first person while dribbling the ball down and back. The action continues until the whole team runs down and back together, while the last person dribbles the ball.

(5) *Ball-o-string:* Each team is given a piece of string or yarn of equal length. Each person on the team must wrap the piece of string around his/her team, unwrap it, and wind it into a ball for the next person.

(6) *May I Have This Dance?:* Each team needs a set of four paper plates. Pairs assume a close dancing position, each with both feet on paper plates, and must dance their way, by sliding their feet, to a marker and back. A frontwards and backwards stance may be used, or have them use a sideways shuffle step.

(7) *Human Chair:* Teammates work in groups of three, with two people clasping hands to form a human chair, and the other person holding their shoulders while riding down to a marker and back. Each person on the team should get a chance to be in all positions.

LET'S GET TOGETHER *(Continued)*

KNOW-AND-GO ACADEMIC RELAYS

Grades: K– 6

Purposes: To combine physical activity with information from various subject areas
To promote teamwork and cooperation

Equipment: Whatever is required for the relays chosen

RELAYS

(1) Content Puzzles: Make tagboard puzzles with numbers, letters, math equations, maps, science vocabulary words, and so forth. Each person on the team must grab a piece of the puzzle at the starting point, run down to a marker, and put one piece of the puzzle in the appropriate place, and then return.

(2) Target Toss Solutions: Make a target on a sheet of paper or with chalk on the ground that has all the letters of the alphabet or the numbers from 0 – 9. Have participants throw one beanbag, ball, or wad of paper each until the team spells the word or gets the numbers to solve the math problem.

(3) Task Card Challenges: Have various tasks in one stack and random numbers in another stack for each team. Each participant must run down, successfully complete the task as many times as the number card indicates, then return. Tasks might include things such as sit-ups, jump rope, forward roll, and so forth. Number cards might be set up as equations to be solved rather than simple numbers.

(4) Body Work: Have individuals or groups use their bodies to form letters, words, or numbers to answer math problems or spell vocabulary words from various subjects.

(5) Alphabet Cards: Make a set of alphabet cards (be sure to make doubles for commonly used letters) or math cards (be careful not to give problems in which a number occurs twice in the answer) for each team. The first person runs to where the cards are stacked, selects the first number or letter in the answer, displays it where the teacher can see it, and runs back to the line and touches the hand of the next person. The round is over when one team spells the word correctly or shows the proper math solution.

KNOW-AND-GO ACADEMIC RELAYS *(Continued)*

LEAD-UP SKILL RELAYS

Grades: K– 6

Purposes: To introduce and reinforce lead-up skills for various sports
To promote teamwork and cooperation

Equipment: Whatever is needed for the activities selected

RELAYS

(1) Basketball: Have teams form a line several feet from the basket. The first person takes one shot from behind the line, gets the rebound, and takes another shot from anywhere, then returns the ball to the next person. Allow three points for a long shot, and one point for a shot from inside the line. The first team to get to the designated point total wins.

(2) Softball: Have teams form lines several feet from a wallboard. Tape a piece of paper or draw a target for each team. Each player throws a ball at the target, retrieves it, and returns it to the next person. Play up to a certain point total, or have each player throw until s/he hits the target, in which case the first team to finish wins.

(3) Soccer: To practice legal throw-ins, have teams form a line with players several feet apart. Teams have a race to see who can use a series of throw-ins to move the ball from person to person, down and back three times. For dribbling practice, set up a course using cones and have participants dribble down and back, then return the ball to the next person in line. To work on shooting, players can dribble to the goal, shoot from a certain distance until they make it, and dribble back to the line. For passing practice, pairs can pass back and forth as they travel to a cone and back.

(4) Football: Teams form lines, and each player must run with the ball to a certain spot, perform a task successfully, and return the ball to the next player. Examples of tasks might be to run to a spot several yards from the goalpost and punt or place kick the ball through the uprights, run to the spot and pass the ball through a suspended hoop or tire, and so forth.

(5) Volleyball: For serving practice, have teams form lines behind the service line and have each person serve and retrieve the ball, then return it to the next person. The requirement might simply be to serve the ball in, or draw a target or place cones in certain areas to make it more challenging. For work on setting, have teams form a line and have every other person face the opposite direction. This will mean that participants will either perform a front set or a back set, as teams try to be first to successfully set the ball up and down the row a few times. For bumping practice, have teams form a line a few feet away from a wallboard. The first person bumps the ball into the wall and quickly gets out of the way. The next person in line must bump the ball into the wall before it hits the ground, and so on, until each person has had a turn.

(6) Combo Drill: Combine all the sports by creating a multisport cross-country event. For example, participants can dribble a basketball to the freethrow line and make one, then dribble a soccer ball through a series of cones, then throw a football until they make it land in a bucket, run the entire base path on the softball field, and hit one successful volleyball serve. Participants should put each piece of equipment back after each event so that it will be in place for the next person.

LEAD-UP SKILL RELAYS *(Continued)*

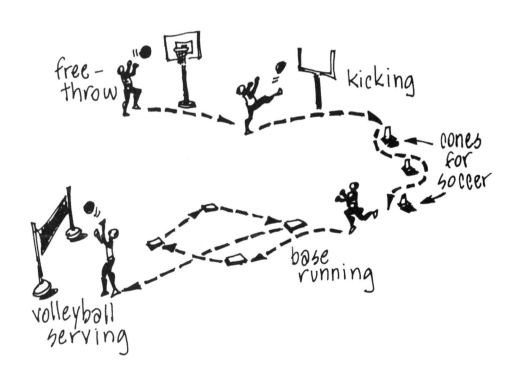

free-throw

kicking

cones for soccer

base running

volleyball serving

H₂O A-GO-GO

Grades: K– 6

Purposes: To get a lot of physical activity, have fun, and cool off on a hot day
To promote cooperation and teamwork

Equipment: Whatever is needed for the relays selected

RELAYS

(1) *Transfer Trot:* Place an empty plastic container several yards away from each team, and a full one (must be much larger) at the starting point. Participants can use a spoon, cup, sponge, or any object to carry water to the empty container. The first team to fill the empty one wins! Add to the challenge by having players carry the cup of water on their head, or between shoulders with pairs, and so forth.

(2) *Squirt Gun Fun:* Put whipped cream on one person from each team. Make a large area on the chest or stomach, or supply goggles and give the person a whipped-cream beard. Each member of the team runs to the person wearing whipped cream, takes two squirts with the squirt gun, and runs back to the line. The first team to remove all the whipped cream wins!

(3) *Slip-n-slide:* Set up two long sheets of plastic, and continue to run water on the Slip-n-slide during the activity. Provide a large T-shirt for each team, and place an empty container at the end of the Slip-n-slide for each group. Participants must put on the shirt, take a turn on the Slip-n-slide, take off the shirt and squeeze all the water into the container, then return the shirt to the next person in line. The first team to fill the container wins!

(4) *Water Balloon Bash:* Fill several water balloons and provide a target for each team. Players run to a marker and toss one water balloon each. The first team to break a certain number of balloons by hitting the target wins. To add to the challenge, have teams form lines with players several feet apart and toss balloons from one player to the next until they reach the person that is throwing at the target. Another fun water balloon relay is to have players run to a marker, pop the balloon by sitting on it, and then return to the line.

(5) *Piggyback Attack:* Have an empty container for each team and have pairs give each other piggyback rides, or have threesomes use a human chair method, while one person carries a cup of water from the starting point and pours what is left at the end of the ride into the empty container. The players then return to the line. The first team to fill the container wins.

(6) *The I'm Not Thirsty Race:* Have a thermos with a spout full of water for each team, and a paper cup for each person. Each participant runs to the thermos, pours and drinks a cup of water, then returns to the line. The first team to empty the thermos wins, and all teams are refreshed!

H₂O A-GO-GO *(Continued)*

VI ACADEMIC ACTION

The following 21 ACADEMIC ACTION games and activities promote cooperation and physical actions to determine subject matter outcomes.

ANIMAL ACTIONS

Grades: K–3

Purposes: To develop large, muscle coordination
To discern the differences in animal movements
To have fun

Equipment: Just the students; however, appropriate sound recordings (for example, jungle sounds, galloping horses, flowing water, and so forth) can enhance the experience

Description: Ask the students how certain animals move. For example, how does a horse move when it walks, trots, prances, jumps, rears up, and/or gallops? Have several students demonstrate and then talk about how the animal moves differently in each situation. Assemble the students in a large circle and tell them that as trained horses they will move around the circle according to your commands. (If you have appropriate sound recordings, begin playing them now.) Start them at a walk for about a minute, then change to a gallop for 30 seconds, then a trot for 2 minutes, then a jump, next "rear up" 2 or 3 times, and so on. To end the activity, have them"freeze" in some position, such as rearing up.

At the next session, select a different animal and discuss its movements. Consider, for example, how a fish moves when at rest, when swimming rapidly through water, when jumping out of water, and when about to prey on smaller fish. When emulating such movements the students might lie on a bench or mat and use their legs as the tail of the fish, their arms as the side fins, and even open and close their mouths as fish do.

During subsequent sessions select a wide variety of animals to repeat the process with. Included might be monkeys, elephants, snakes, camels, ducks, eagles, cats, dogs, and so forth.

Variations: (1) The opportunity to learn about lesser known animals can result from this activity. For example how do ocelots, wombats, pronghorns, or narwhals move? In fact, if notified in advance of the rare animal, the students may wish to do research; the teacher, in turn, might locate related pictures, articles, books, films, or computer simulations. (2) The students might also move in the fashion of machines. As such they might become robots (which most will have seen on TV) or such other mechanical devices as trash compactors, vacuum cleaners, steam shovels, or automobile jacks.

ANIMAL ACTIONS (Continued)

BIG FOOT RELAY

Grades: K–3

Purposes: To develop measurement understandings
To enhance flexibility and balance

Equipment: Purchase several sets of the largest size men's thongs (12" long) at a discount store or make cardboard feet cutouts. (See the pattern that follows.) Use rubber bands to attach the cardboard feet to the students' shoes

Description: With students' help measure the thongs (or cardboard feet) to certify that they are one foot (12 inches) long. Also mark goal lines on the playing field a selected distance apart, such as 100 feet. Next, organize the pupils into several equal teams, with half of each team waiting behind each of the goal lines. The first member of each team puts on thongs (or cardboard feet) and at the start signal walks in a heel-to-toe fashion as rapidly as s/he can to the opposite goal. As soon as s/he crosses the goal line another member of the team starts the heel to toe relay in the opposite direction. The relay continues until all players have completed their segment of the Big Foot Relay.

Variations: Students might also take part in a *Jolly Green Giant Relay* where giant feet cutouts are one yard (or one meter) long. As such, the students work in pairs with each attaching a single giant foot to one of his/her shoes. One partner places her giant foot with the heel to the goal line, the partner walks or hops forward until his giant foot touches the toe of hers, and so forth. (If this proves too difficult, the student may carry and place the giant feet with their hands.) Play continues in this manner until all student partners have traveled a set distance, such as 100 yards.

BIG FOOT RELAY *(Continued)*

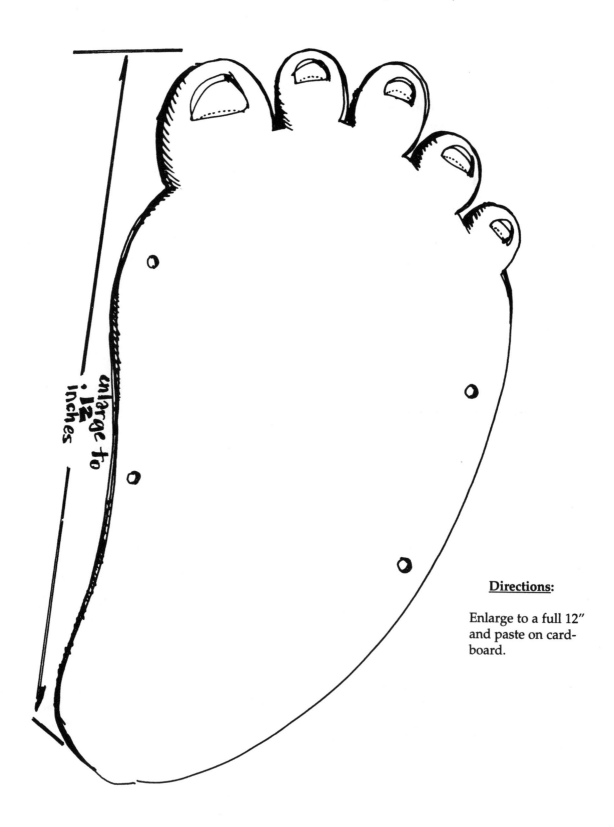

enlarge to 12 inches

Directions:

Enlarge to a full 12″ and paste on cardboard.

TOSS AND ANSWER

Grades: K–6

Purposes: To provide for a focused review of any subject
To enhance throwing skills
To improve mental and verbal quickness

Equipment: A balloon (or very light weight scarf) plus pencil and paper for each pair of students

Description: One student holds a balloon which s/he is ready to toss as high as possible. Her opponent stands ready to verify and record the outcome. The teacher then calls out a question or problem and states TOSS AND ANSWER! The balloon holder immediately tosses the balloon as high as s/he can and attempts to answer the question as fully as possible before the balloon touches the ground. She and her opponent verify the outcome together and it is recorded. The players then change roles and the teacher calls out a new problem to TOSS AND ANSWER. After an equal number of questions, the correct responses for each player are totaled. If a winning team is to be designated, the player totals are added together.

A wide variety of questions or problems are possible. Young students might be asked to count as high as they can before the balloon touches the ground. Students who have studied the skeletal system might be asked to touch the location of and give the proper name for as many of the bones of their own bodies as they can. Other students who are attempting to master multiplication facts could be told to begin with $7 \times 1 = 7$ and recite as many of the 7's facts as they can before the balloon drops. Utilize content from all the subject areas being studied and have fun reviewing with TOSS AND ANSWER.

Variations: (1) Young children might do this activity in groups with all answering together; it is not necessary to keep a written record. (2) For questions with long answers or more complex problems, students might be allowed to bat the balloon into the air repeatedly and continue to answer for an extended time.

TOSS AND ANSWER (Continued)

YARN ART PATTERNS

Grades: K–6

Purposes: To actively create large yarn art designs
To cooperatively predict and check outcomes
To discern mathematical patterns in art designs
To enhance throwing and catching skills

Equipment: Several balls of yarn (or string) and some chalk

Description: To demonstrate how this activity works, begin by having 10 students space themselves evenly around a large playground circle. (If a circle with a diameter of at least 10 ft. is not available, use the yarn and chalk to draw one.) Once spaced evenly, use the chalk to number the student positions; begin with 0 and continue to 9, as shown in the diagram below. Give Student 0 a ball of yarn, have him or her hold the end and pass the ball along to Student 1, Student 2, and so on until it gets back to Student 0. Then have the students determine how many sides their yarn figure has. (Visualizing the figure is sometimes easier if the yarn is placed on the ground and held snugly.) Also, ask them if they know the name of this polygon. Roll the yarn back on the ball and get ready for the next phase of this activity.

The second phase again starts with Student 0, but this time the yarn is to be thrown in multiples of 2; that is, the yarn will go from 0 to 2, to 4, to 6, to 8, and back to 0. Can the students predict the outcome? Have the group throw the yarn, determine the number of sides in this new design and name the polygon.

In phase three, as multiples of 3 are connected, something new will happen. Have the students guess likely outcomes. Then, beginning again with 0, throw the yarn ball to 3, to 6, to 9, to 2, to 5, and on until 0 is reached again. Stretch this new yarn art design on the ground and discuss what happened.

Try the activity for multiples of 4; that is, toss from 0 to 4, to 8, and on until 0 is reached. What different yarn art design will you get? What happens with multiples of 5? What of multiples of 6 or 7, and so forth? Are there any different multiples that yield the same pattern? Why?

Variations: (1) Less complex tasks for young students might have them use the yarn to create basic shapes such as squares, rectangles, and triangles. (2) Older students (if successful with the activities noted above) should repeat the process, but with circles utilizing different numbers of student locations. For example, try to predict and create other Yarn Art Designs when 8 students are evenly spaced around the large circle; or try 7 students, or any number. (Note: when using more students a larger circle is necessary and generally a greater quantity of yarn will be needed.) (3) Advanced students might consider further focuses as the length of uniform sides, the degree measurement of the vertex angles, and so forth.

YARN ART PATTERNS (Continued)

Decagon

Pentagon

multiples of three

multiples of four

yarn.

GIANT TANGRAM CREATURES

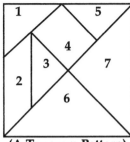

(A Tangram Pattern)

Grades: K– 6

Purposes: To actively create large tangram art creatures
To utilize both logical and creative thinking skills
To have fun

Equipment: Large pieces of cardboard (for example, refrigerator boxes which will be cut into specified shapes) and several boxes of colored chalk

Description: At the onset, large tangram pieces need to be cut from cardboard (as large as feasible) and labeled 1 through 7, as shown above. Cut enough tangram sets so that each student will have a piece or two to work with. (Note: Allow upper grade students to mark and cut out the tangram sets. It will provide a good learning experience for them.)

Organize the students into cooperative groups of four to seven students. Within each group each student will participate using a tangram piece or two. The first job for each group will be to carry their seven pieces to a new location and attempt to reassemble them (without looking at a pattern) into the original square shape; when assembled they should chalk around all their pieces and show this to the leader to prove success. The next jobs might be to use the triangle cutouts as follows: (1) use any two triangles to create a square, (2) next use three triangles to make a square, and (3) create still another square by utilizing four triangles. The students might also explore and keep a record of additional standard geometric shapes they created with two, or three, or more tangram parts.

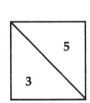
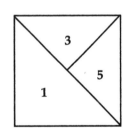
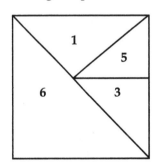

The logical thinking activities, noted above, are of genuine interest to students, but what they really enjoy are creating Giant Tangram Creatures. Such creatures are created by placing at least four, and preferably all seven, of the pieces on the playground to form a creature image. The pieces may be arranged and rearranged until the entire group agrees that it resembles the creature that they are attempting to represent. Their creature might emulate a real animal such as a giraffe, or a fictional creature like a dragon, or a robotic creature, and so on. When satisfied, they are to trace around the cardboard tangram pieces and then set them aside. Next they are to use the colored chalk to shade their creature and to give it features; if a giraffe is their selected creature, they would likely color in the eyes, mouth, hooves, and a bristly mane as well as its many spots. When all of the groups have finished, take time to examine and discuss each Giant Tangram Creature; each student might make one comment as to why their group selected a particular creature, the process of assembling the tangram pieces, the way they decided to color their creature, and so forth.

GIANT TANGRAM CREATURES *(Continued)*

Variations: (1) Several groups might be allowed to use their tangram pieces together to create an exceptionally large creature (for example, a snake the length of the playground). (2) Students working at advanced levels could consider the wealth of mathematical vocabulary associated with tangrams (for example, parallel, perpendicular, bisect, congruent, similar, ratio, proportion, or symmetry).

FOOD FOR SURVIVAL

Grades: K– 6

Purposes: To simulate the food requirements of all animals
To develop careful observation skills and agility
To better understand the balance of nature

Equipment: Sack of 500 or more kernels of dry corn or beans

Description: To remain healthy and survive, all animals (as well as human beings) must have access to an adequate food supply. In this simulation the students play the part of individual animals in a herd, flock, or school; they might be fish, deer, geese, and so forth.

The teacher begins the activity by broadcasting the food (corn or beans) onto the playing field and notes that each animal must obtain a specified amount of food per week (assume 4 kernels) to remain healthy. At a signal the animals (students) run and collect 4 kernels for their first week's food. These kernels are returned to the sack and a signal to search for food for the second week is given. Every animal will likely find enough food for the first few weeks, but as the food supply becomes more limited only 3, 2, or 1 kernel(s) may be obtained. If an animal finds only 3 kernels for 2 consecutive weeks, he or she becomes weak and can no longer run, but must walk to try and find food for the next week. If only 2 kernels are found, the animal is further weakened and must walk while holding onto an ankle with one hand. Finding only 1 kernel forces a slow crawl; and if 1 or 0 kernels are found for more than 3 consecutive weeks, the animal dies and must remain on the ground.

The Food for Survival simulation continues for a designated time. The time might be a specified number of weeks, or until winter is past, or a drought is over, or the size of the herd is decimated to the point where the population can again be fed adequately.

FOOD FOR SURVIVAL *(Continued)*

Variations: (1) For young students, the simulation might be modified to cite the importance of feeding pets the proper amount and kind of food per day. (2) Older students might consider the long term effects of whether their society should decide to feed a starving herd during winter months. In such an instance, the teacher might provide supplemental feedings by scattering additional kernels of food onto the field.

ARM LOCK MATH

Grades: K– 6

Purposes: To act out mathematical computations
To foster cooperation
To correlate applied and abstract math

Equipment: Chalk

Description: Demonstrate how the activity is to work by writing a number, such as 7, on the blacktop with chalk. Select 7 students and ask them to choose and state an addition combination that equals 7. They might note, for example, that 4 + 3 = 7. Use the chalk to write that equation on the playground and then direct the group to show it; that is, 4 students are to form one group by linking arms while the remaining 3 students form a separate group. Next, ask 7 more students to choose, write with chalk and act out a different addition combination for 7 (e.g. 5 + 2 or 6 + 1 or even 7 +0).

For more advanced students select problems like 29 ÷ 8 = ____. After this computation problem is written with chalk, have the students note that 29 people are to be put in groups of 8. Then let the 29 students arrange themselves and link arms such that they end up with three groups of 8 and a remainder of 5 people whose arms are not linked. (*Note:* the students might also be made aware that 29 ÷ 8 = _____ may be considered as 29 split into 8 groups with 3 students linked per group and, since there are not enough additional people to put another in each group, there exists a remainder of 5 unlinked students.)

4+2=6

ARM LOCK MATH *(Continued)*

Variations: (1) In order to comprehend fully addition or subtraction number combinations, young students may need to touch and count the arm-locked students on a 1 to 1 basis. (2) Subtraction combinations might be portrayed by having the subtracted students sit down (or even be hidden behind a backstop or around the corner of a building). (3) Advanced students might portray equations which call for use of the proper order of operations; that is, parentheses, exponents, multiply, divide, add, and subtract in order from left to right. For example, $10 + 6 - 3 \times 4$ should be treated as $(10 + 6) - (3 \times 4) = 4$; it is, in fact, a good idea to chalk the parenthesis marks on the playground surface between the affected arm-locked students.

POST-IT MATH

Grades: K– 6

Purposes: To physically act out mathematical computations
To provide for mental calculations
To stimulate logical thinking

Equipment: Large size Post-It-Notes (or index cards and masking tape) and a marking pen

Description: The leader secretly writes single digit numerals on two Post-It-Notes (or use index cards and masking tape) and places them on the back of a selected player. The selected player then turns his/her back to the other group members, so that they may see the numbers which he/she cannot, and then turns to face the group again. The leader next calls upon the group to complete certain physical activities based on the two Post-It numbers, and it is the job of the selected player to figure out and state what numbers are posted on his/her back.

Assume that the two Post-It numerals are 3 and 8. The leader might first call on the group members to hop (perhaps on one foot) the sum of the numbers and count 1, 2, 3 . . . 11 in unison. The selected player is then allowed one guess as to which numerals are on his/her back; if s/he answers correctly the round is over and a new selected player is chosen, but, if not the leader calls for another physical activity with the two numbers. For example, the leader might call on the group members to show the product of the numbers by running in place and counting in unison 1, 2, 3 . . . 24 for each time their right foot touches the ground. If necessary, this round of Post-It Math might continue by acting out the difference between the two numbers or even the quotient (for example, by completing 2-2/3 push-ups). If the selected player is able to guess the correct numerals with two tries s/he gets to name the new selected player; if not the leader makes the selection.

POST-IT MATH *(Continued)*

Variations: (1) Beginners might work with a single numeral and initially just practice acting out that number value. Later they might play *One Less* where the acted out number value is one less than the number on the selected player's back; that is, if the group members complete 7 jumps, the selected player must say 8 to be correct (other options include Two Less, One More, and so forth). (2) When played for spelling, a word is posted on the selected student's back and s/he must try to guess the word from group clues to individual letters. Given the word Compose, for example, the students in the group must first pantomime the letter C, and as soon as s/he guesses correctly everyone jumps into the air with both hands raised high. Each letter is pantomimed (if helpful, students may team up to form letters) in turn until s/he guesses the word and is able to correctly spell it aloud.

GRAB + RACE + SPELL

Grades: K–6

Purposes: To actively practice spelling
To enhance hand coordination and running skills
To foster mental recall and team cooperation

Equipment: Several hundred plastic or cardboard letters, or alphabet letters printed on discs or other small objects, and a container to hold them all. (If needed, students can bring caps to gallon milk containers from home and print a letter on each with magic markers.) A dictionary or thesaurus might also be helpful

Description: Equal teams of 4 or 5 students compete by taking one turn each to grab a handful of letters, run to a goal position, and then arrange their team's letters to spell as many words as possible. This procedure may be timed (usually from 2 to 5 minutes are required) or the teams may be allowed to seek more words or higher scoring words until a designated signal.

When completion is noted by any team (that team might stand with arms folded) the leader blows a whistle, allows 30 seconds for the other teams to finish, and then blows the whistle a second time for all activity to stop. The spelled words are then examined by all the teams and the leader for accuracy. Any words spelled incorrectly are eliminated; use a dictionary or thesaurus to settle disputes. The rest of the words are scored on a predetermined basis such as 1 point for each of the first five letters utilized per word and 2 points for each additional letter, minus a point for each unused letter.

Variations: (1) Allow young students to place all of the As together, all Bs together, and so on, and/or to place the letters in alphabetical order. (2) Older students might be required to spell words with a minimum of three or four letters. (3) Bonus points might be awarded to the fastest running teams and/or to teams with the longest words (for instance, 8 points for the fastest or longest, 7 points for the next best, 6 for the next, and so forth).

SCRAMBLE TO WIN

Grades: K– 6

Purposes: To provide for the reinforcement of mathematical computation or spelling/vocabulary reviews

To foster quick decision making
To enhance running skills

Equipment: Math reinforcement activities call for a set of cards numbered 0 through 9 for each team of ten players (each set of cards should be a different color). Spelling/vocabulary reviews require several sets of alphabet cards for each team

Description: To play mathematical Scramble to Win organize the students into teams of ten and give each player a number card (players with blue number cards are on the blue team, those with pink cards are a team, and so forth). If the number of students doesn't allow for even teams of ten, capable students might be given two cards or assigned jobs as scorekeeper or judge. When ready to begin, the leader calls out a math problem. Each student solves the problem mentally (or with pencil and paper) and checks to see whether his or her number card is part of the answer. Players having correct answer numerals run to a designated location and display their cards in proper order, as viewed by the leader. A point is awarded to each team displaying the correct answer, plus a bonus point is scored by the team that was both first and correct.

Spelling/vocabulary Scramble to Win is played in a similar manner, but certain format modifications are necessary. In this setting alphabet cards are placed in stacks (all As together, all Bs, and so on) at each team location (ten or more members per team) and each member is responsible for designated letters. When ready to begin, the leader calls for a spelling word (or states a vocabulary definition) and sets a time limit, such as twenty seconds. During the time limit, the team members must decide quickly how to spell the word (plus, if a definition was stated, what the word is), who will run with the first letter, the second, and so forth. When the time limit is up, the leader says, "First Runner Go," pauses about three seconds, then says, "Second Runner Go," pauses another three seconds, "Third Runner Go," and continues until Stop is called. Each team's players, in turn, run to their designated locations, where they attempt to show their cards in proper spelling order. Scoring, if desired, is on the basis of one point for each letter placed correctly.

Variations: (1) Young players might begin by just finding a correct number or letter and running to a designated location. (2) For more able students, increase the difficulty level by stating problems that require fraction or decimal answers (decimal point cards will be needed). (3) Call for answers from other subject areas. For example, "Lake Superior borders on three states; name one of them." A correct response would require that they spell out Minnesota, Wisconsin, or Michigan.

SCRAMBLE TO WIN (Continued)

STOP AND GO MUSICAL HOOPS

Grades: K– 6

Purposes: To practice moving to musical rhythms
To learn to appreciate different types of music
To exercise vigorously for several short time periods

Equipment: 10 or more hula hoops (or circles may be chalked on the playground), 30 or more index cards (exercise directions need to be prewritten on them), and a variety of recorded music (to enhance the school collection, students should be encouraged to bring their favorite music to class) plus playback equipment

Description: Set the hula hoops in a large circle on the playground. In each, place 3 or more index cards with the exercise directions face down. (Hop on 1 foot, Jumping jacks, Push-ups, Run in place, Knee bends, Touch your toes)

Have the students space themselves into a large circle just outside the hula hoops. Play a musical selection for 1 or 2 minutes, note the rhythm, and have several students demonstrate how they might move (for example, walking, skipping, waltzing, trotting, or galloping) in time to the music. Select one type of movement, perhaps skipping, and when the music begins again have everyone skip in a clockwise direction for 2 or 3 minutes. As soon as the music stops everyone must get into the nearest hoop, turn over a card, and rapidly do the indicated exercise for 1 minute. When the music begins again, the students resume their large circle positions, the leader states a new rhythm movement, perhaps trotting, and again, everyone moves in time to the music. The sequence of 1 minute of vigorous exercise followed by 3 minutes of rhythm movement is repeated several times. Then switch to a different type of music (classical, rock and roll, jazz, waltz, country, twist,) and continue the sequence.

Variations: (1) The music for young students should have a definite beat; in fact, the leader may want to emphasize it by beating on a drum. Also, young learners might all do the same vigorous exercise as called out by the leader. (2) If appropriate, older students might complete the rhythm portions as line or couple dances.

STOP AND GO MUSICAL HOOPS *(Continued)*

VERB ACTIONS

Grades: K– 6

Purposes: To physically demonstrate action verbs
To enhance small and/or large muscle coordination
To foster mental recall and cooperative group decisions

Equipment: Index cards with action verbs written on them may be used initially. No other materials are needed; however, readily available school or playground equipment may be utilized

Description: Explain (or review) the fact that most verbs express some kind of action; they express doing, becoming, or happening. Then organize the students as cooperative groups of 3, 4, or 5 students and note that each group will, in turn, be acting out their verbs silently.

For the first round have each group act out a verb that may be discerned readily (for example, run or kick). After one group has acted out their verb the other groups need to decide cooperatively what they think the verb was. As soon as a group has decided they are to give a silent signal (such as standing with their arms folded). The leader then asks each group what verb they think was portrayed. If the activity is to be scored, wait until all groups have answered, and then award a point for each correct response; a bonus point might also be awarded to the first group giving the silent signal. (*Note:* The verb *knock* is portrayed in the following illustration; as *to knock on a door*. Strike or hit might also be acceptable synonyms.)

Variations: (1) Select short verbs that are easily acted out by young learners and print them on index cards; if they are not yet able to read, whisper the verb in each player's ear. (2) Have advanced students try to portray more subtle verbs (such as laugh, think, or collide).

I HAVE ___, WHO HAS ___?

Grades: K– 6

Purposes: To provide focused reviews of any subject
To enhance listening skills
To provide for mild exercise

Equipment: Cards on which the I HAVE ___, WHO HAS ___? clues are written

Description: The leader needs to prepare sequential clue cards in advance; *see* examples below. Players assemble behind a starting line and one card is distributed to each randomly. The leader stands opposite them behind the answer line and says, "Ready! When you think you have the answer to a clue, you must hop on one foot (or another designated physical task) to the answer line, and state I HAVE ___ (answer)___. If we agree that you are correct, you will then read the clue on the bottom of your card which says WHO HAS ___? Some other player will need to hop to the finish line and see if she or he can correctly say I HAVE ___ (answer) ___. The game is finished when everyone has correctly crossed the answer line and the final clue is answered by me."

To illustrate, a multiplication practice game (for only 5 players) might include the cards shown below. As such, the leader would start by stating I HAVE _100_, WHO HAS 5 X 7? The player whose card has the correct answer would need to hop on one foot to the answer line and state loudly I HAVE _35_. All that agree 5 X 7 = 35 should signal a correct answer, perhaps by jumping high into the air with both hands raised. Then, that player calls out WHO HAS 7 X 8? Another student hops forward to state I HAVE _56_. Should more than one student hop forward, the group must determine which answer is correct; any incorrect player must hop back to the starting line. Play continues in this manner until the final player has answered correctly and asks WHO HAS 10 X 10? The leader, of course, answers I HAVE _100_.

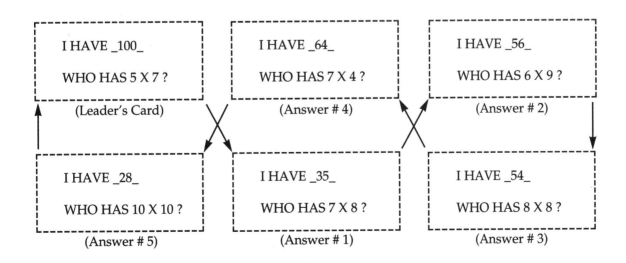

I HAVE ___ , WHO HAS ___? *(Continued)*

I HAVE ___ , WHO HAS ___ games can readily be devised for most subject reviews. Spelling, for example, might include questions as WHO HAS E-N-O-U-G-H?; the student with the answer must pronounce the word correctly as she says I HAVE ENOUGH. A possible Social Studies question might be WHO HAS THE CAPITOL OF CALIFORNIA? (Sacramento) A vocabulary question could be WHO HAS THE WORD MEANING TO HOLD BACK OR KEEP FROM GOING ON? (detain) Such questions should, of course, be age appropriate.

Variations: (1) Young students might make motions which the players must interpret. For example, instead of the question WHO HAS 6?, the student might instead say WHO HAS and then use his hands to CLAP, CLAP, CLAP, CLAP, CLAP, CLAP. (2) Advanced students might each be given several cards. As such, they might hop to the answer line for their first correct response, skip back to the start line for a second correct answer, run again to the answer line for a third positive reply, and so forth.

SCIENCE/MATH SCAVENGER HUNT

Grades: 4 – 6

Purposes: To reinforce science and/or math understandings
To develop observation skills and agility
To encourage cooperative group work

Equipment: School and playground items, questions prepared in advance, plus paper and pencils to record responses

Description: The students might be lined up in random order and then numbered off 1 through 8. The 1's make up the first cooperative group, the 2's another group, and so on. Within each group it is also a good idea to prescribe roles as director, encourager, recorder, and reporter. However, regardless of their roles, all group members will attempt to search out the scavenger hunt items.
  Once organized, the groups are given a list of science and/or math items to search for, all procedures to be followed are noted, and a specified amount of time is designated. The science/math objects to be located (with potential answers) might include, for example, the following:

1. Anything with 6 legs (insect; some benches or tables)

2. Something cylindrical in shape (tree trunk; metal fence posts)

3. Anything that contains pigment (paint; most anything of color)

4. Something that displays reflective symmetry (butterfly wings; some window panes)

5. Something that occurs in 2s (eyes; ropes on a swing)

6. Objects with acute angles (fingers spread; most tree branches)

7. Something that occurs in 5s (human toes; some clusters of leaves)

8. Anything having clay in it (brick; some soils)

9. Something that has a mass close to 10 grams (small rock; large leaf)

10. Two objects with different shapes, but the same perimeter (different types of leaves; a metal pipe or a tree trunk)

Allow perhaps 20 minutes for each group to locate as many different solution objects as possible. Set aside another 5 to 10 minutes for the recorders to organize the list for their team. Spend some time discussing the items located for each question and agreeing as to accuracy. Then, if scoring is to be done, award 2 points for the first correct answer to each question and 1 point for each additional item; the greatest point value wins.

Variations: (1) Questions for young learners should be age appropriate as "What things are necessary for plants to grow?" (soil, water, sunshine). (2) Advanced learners might attempt to "locate isosceles triangles in nature" (vein structure in certain leaves).

SCIENCE/MATH SCAVENGER HUNT *(Continued)*

SCIENCE FREEZE TAG

Grades: 4 – 6

Purposes: To reinforce science understandings
To enhance quickness and agility
To encourage quick thinking

Equipment: Items available at the school playground; also, questions prepared in advance are helpful

Description: The teacher or leader calls out a science question and the players are required to answer by touching only (anyone talking is disqualified). Sample questions and potential responses might include, "Can you touch something that has chlorophyll in it?" (grass) or "Can you find something that is made with iron and a little carbon?" (chain link fence) or "Can you locate a vertebrate and touch the part which shows that you are certain of your answer?" (touch their own or another player's backbone). After a designated time a signal is given and all players must "freeze" in position; any players not touching an answer item must complete a designated physical activity (for instance, run in place, do sit-ups, stand with both hands high in the air).

Discuss their answers and note all correct solutions. If score keeping is desired, it may be done individually or in teams. For individual scoring have each person carry a pencil and an index card upon which they record a tally for each of their own correct responses. Team scoring is done in the same manner except that a point is awarded for each member with a correct response; a bonus point might also be awarded if the entire team had correct responses. When ready, continue with another question.

Variations: (1) Questions for young learners should be age appropriate, such as "Can you touch something that might be fed to cows?" (grass). (2) Advanced learners might attempt to locate a hard, amorphous, brittle, usually transparent surface (glass).

DIRECTION RUN

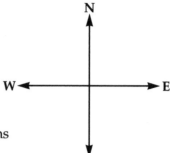

Grades: 4 – 6

Purposes: To physically demonstrate knowledge of map directions
To enhance running skills and agility
To carefully follow written clues

Equipment: A large map of the school playground, cards of different colors with sequential clues for each team, and chalk

Description: Discuss the use of directions north, south, east, and west as they apply to map reading in general and specifically to the school playground map. (Advanced learners might also deal with more complex settings as northeast or south southwest.) Tell the students that they will be applying their map reading skills to a playground running game; that is, each team will run a sort of relay according to prewritten direction clues. The teacher or leader will want to write out the Direction Run card clues and tape them in place in advance; a North, East, South, West direction indicator can also be chalked on the playground near the starting location.

When ready, divide the class into equal teams (for example, 4 teams each with 7 players) and do a trial run. If there are 7 players on each team, the prewritten clues must include 8 direction locations, plus a position that all students begin from. As such, the team members must find all 8 locations in relay fashion, but they will do so in different sequences. For example, the first clue, which the teacher hands to a Blue Team player might state "Go to the northwestern corner of the playground and find instructions on a blue card." As soon as that player locates the blue card she raises her hand high and a second member of the Blue Team runs to confer with her/him. That second player receives the instructions that tell him to "Find your next clue under the equipment on the South end of the playground." He leaves player 1 at the first location and runs to try and locate the second clue. Play continues in this manner, with a new team player joining the relay each time a clue is located, until all clues have been found and acted on.

While the Blue Team is trying to find their clues and rapidly complete the Direction Run the other teams are also doing so, but arriving at the clue locations in different sequences. For example, the first instruction to Green Team member might be "Find your clue on a green card under the equipment on the South end of the playground." (Notice that this was the second location the Blue Team was to arrive at.) That Green Team player would then find a card stating "Go to the northwestern corner of the playground and find instructions on a green card," which he/she would pass on to his/her relay team member, and so on. The first team to place a relay team member at all Direction Run locations successfully wins the round.

Variations: (1) Measurement tasks can be included by giving such clues as "Go 45 meters northwest for your next instruction." (2) Students familiar with the concept of degrees in a circle might receive instructions such as "Face to the south, turn 90 degrees clockwise, and proceed to the edge of the playground."

DIRECTION RUN *(Continued)*

SPIDER WEB DEFINITIONS

Grades: 4 – 6

Purposes: To create a yarn spider web
To review important information
To enhance throwing and catching skills

Equipment: Several balls of yarn or string and one or more sets of review questions with matching definitions

Description: Have 8 or more students hold hands and space themselves arms length apart in a circle. Give one student a ball of yarn and begin by having the teacher or leader call out a question such as, "What is a long, narrow valley with high cliffs on each side called?" Wait a few seconds for the other students to signal whether they know the answer. The student with the yarn ball then calls on someone to state the answer; in this instance "canyon" is a correct answer. If correct, the first student holds onto the loose end and throws the ball to the answering student. Continue to build the Spider Web by asking another question and then throwing the yarn ball to a third student who has signaled that s/he knows the answer. Repeat the process until everyone has at least one hold on the yarn and/or all of the yarn ball has been unrolled.

When rolling the yarn back into a ball, begin with the last student and reverse the process. That is, state a definition and have the preceding student provide the related information. For example, if vocabulary and spelling were focuses, the leader might state, "Spell the word that means the use of irony, sarcasm, and humor to criticize or make fun of something bad or foolish." The student should then spell "s-a-t-i-r-e" and reroll that segment of the yarn; however, if s/he isn't able to answer, s/he may call on another student to help. Continue in this manner until all of the yarn is rerolled into a ball.

SPIDER WEB DEFINITIONS *(Continued)*

Variations: (1) Young students might roll, rather than throw, the yarn ball and their questions should be age appropriate; for example, "If 2 birds are sitting on a wire and 1 more joins them, how many birds are now sitting on the wire?" (2) Advanced students might answer questions that require sequential responses; that is, the teacher might state, "Begin with 7, add 8, multiply by 3, divide by 15, double that, and add your number of fingers and toes." A student, in turn, should answer "15" and have the yarn ball tossed to him, "45" and another student gets the yarn ball, "3" and s/he receives the ball. Continue in this fashion until out of yarn.

STATE (OR COUNTRY) RACE

Grades: 4 – 6

Purposes: To reinforce geography and social studies understandings
To enhance large and small muscle coordination

Equipment: A large outline map of the United States (or the countries of the world) painted on the blacktop, and prewritten questions

Description: Divide the class into even teams and line up at a starting location that is about 20 ft. from the large outline map. Ask a question relating to a specific map location, allow approximately 30 seconds for each team to confer as to what they think the solution is, and signal "go." At the "go" command, the first student on each team runs to the map and places a foot on the location his or her team decides is the correct answer. When "stop" is signaled, have the runners remain in position and conduct a brief discussion regarding the solution(s). If scoring is to take place, 1 point might be given to each team with a correct answer, plus a bonus point awarded to the team whose player was first to reach a correct destination.

Any appropriate questions might be asked. For example:

1. Can you locate a state that shares a border with Mexico? (Texas, New Mexico, Arizona, and/or California)

2. Which is known as the "Show Me" state? (Missouri)

3. The smallest of the 50 states is _____? (Rhode Island)

Questions that relate to the world (and solutions) might include:

1. Which is the smallest continent in the world? (Australia)

2. This country is known as the "Switzerland of Latin America"? (Costa Rica)

3. Which countries are sometimes called the Baltic States? (Lithuania, Latvia, and Estonia)

Variations: (1) In the classroom, the same type of information can be portrayed by utilizing large wall maps, globes, and reference materials. 2) A list of potential questions might be supplied in advance so that the students can prepare for an upcoming *State (or Country) Run.* (3) Additional physical activity might be incorporated by requiring the students to skip rope 10 times before running or jump over obstacles on the way, and so forth.

STATE (OR COUNTRY) RACE *(Continued)*

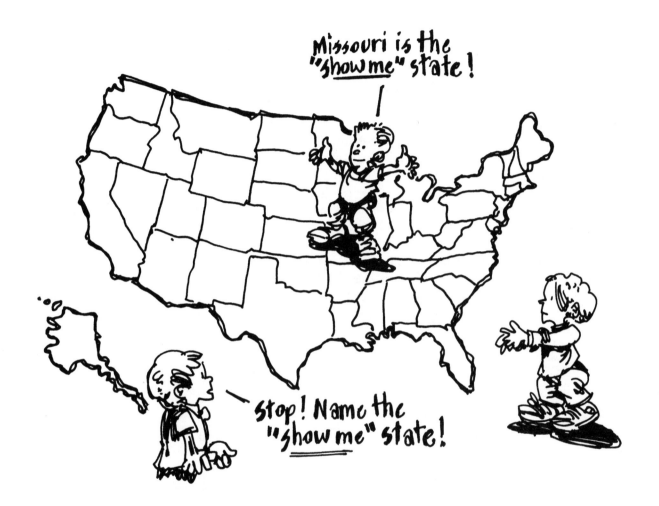

ROPE FENCES

Grades: 4 – 6

Purposes: To physically create and map fenced areas
To work in cooperative groups
To discover relationships between perimeters and areas
To predict logical outcomes

Equipment: Several lengths of rope or string from 8 to 40 feet, a 1 foot square cardboard for each student, chalk, tape, and such available measuring devices as yard sticks, 1 foot rulers, and a measurement trundle wheel (optional)

Description: Prior to beginning the activity, ask the students what the terms square, rectangle, square foot, perimeter, and area mean; help them to clarify any concepts not fully understood. Then use the 8 foot rope to demonstrate what they will be doing. Tape the rope to the playground in a square and ask what the perimeter is and what the area is. Have the students use foot rulers or yardsticks to measure the perimeter as 2′ + 2′ + 2′ + 2′ = 8 ft. The area should then be determined by placing four of the 1 sq. ft. cardboards inside the rope fence. Have the students note that the square with an 8 ft. perimeter has an area of 4 sq. ft.; it is also a good idea to have these and subsequent findings recorded for future use.

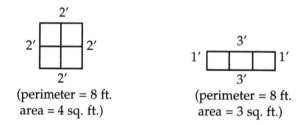

(perimeter = 8 ft.
area = 4 sq. ft.)

(perimeter = 8 ft.
area = 3 sq. ft.)

Next, have the students use the same rope to create a rectangle measuring 1′ x 3′ x 1′ x 3′. Instruct them to measure the perimeter and to use cardboard squares to find the area. They will discover that the perimeter is still 8 ft., but that the area now measures only 3 sq. ft. Ask them to explain why, when the perimeter remained constant, the areas were different.

Now it is time to organize the students into working groups of 4 or more. Have them construct, measure, and record their findings for a variety of Rope Fences. (Good rope lengths are 8, 12, 16, 20, 24, 28, 32, 36 and 40 ft.; diagrams for 16 ft. Rope Fences are shown below.) Furthermore, note that all measurements are to be in 1 ft. increments. Finally, tell them to be ready to share their findings.

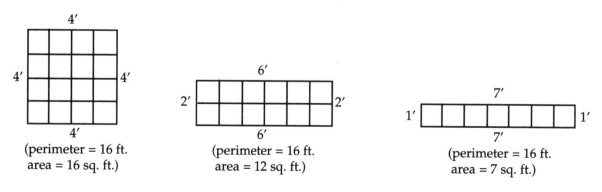

(perimeter = 16 ft.
area = 16 sq. ft.)

(perimeter = 16 ft.
area = 12 sq. ft.)

(perimeter = 16 ft.
area = 7 sq. ft.)

ROPE FENCES (Continued)

Variations: (1) A trundle wheel might be used to measure large perimeters and the area square footage might be drawn with chalk instead of using cardboard squares. (2) Have the students predict outcomes they think will result for a longer rope, perhaps 100 ft. Have them construct the Rope Fences and compare them with their estimates. (3) Advanced students might attempt Rope Fences with circles and/or other nonrectangular shapes; it will likely be necessary to estimate and combine portions of sq. ft.

COORDINATE FRISBEE (OR BEANBAG) TOSS

Grades: 4 – 6

Purposes: To determine coordinate locations
To enhance hand/eye coordination
To practice math skills

Equipment: Several Frisbees, beanbags, or paper plates, 30 or more cards with different coordinate locations listed (such as (5,0) or (2,7)), masking tape, chalk, paint, or small markers to denote graph locations

Description: Mark the playing field into positive quadrant coordinate graph locations as shown in the diagram below. Use a long tape measure, rope, or string to help locate the numbered locations which should be a yard (or a meter) apart. The markings should be semipermanent to allow for repeated use of the activity. (*Note:* it is recommended that upper-grade students construct this field as a combined study of mathematics and sports.)

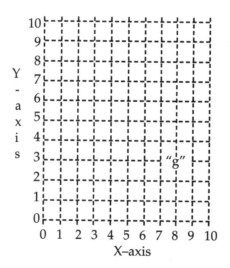

Note: Read the X-axis number first, and then the Y-axis position. For example, the location noted as "g" should be read as (8,3).

Teams of four students draw one card each from the coordinate deck. At their team's turn, all four team members stand near (0,0) and toss their Frisbees so that they will, hopefully, land on the coordinate locations noted on their respective cards. Each team member then stands at his/her designated location and displays the card for everyone to see. The individual then states his/her score for that throw—3 points if the Frisbee is touching the coordinate, 2 points if it is within a foot of the location, or 1 point if it is farther away—and if all concur, it is added to a cumulative team score. The winning team is the one that has the greatest score after a set number of rounds.

COORDINATE FRISBEE (OR BEANBAG) TOSS *(Continued)*

Variations: (1) Use bean bags or paper plates instead of Frisbees. 2) Have the throws made from such different locations as (0,7), (10,9), or (8,2). (3) For young students one axis might show letters; thus locations would appear as (B,4), (F,8), and so forth. (4) Use a four quadrant coordinate grid with older students.

NUMBER POWER ACTIONS

Grades: 4 – 6

Purposes: To conceptualize mathematical number powers
To act out the powers of numbers physically
To stimulate logical thinking

Equipment: None, unless precise measurements are desired; then measuring devices such as yard (or meter) sticks, long tapes and/or trundle wheels, and chalk can be utilized

Description: Be certain that students understand that a *power* of a number is the product obtained by multiplying the number by itself a given number of times. For example, to *square* a number such as 3 (also called raising a number to its *second power*) means to treat it as 3^2 or 3 X 3 which yields 9. Likewise, 3^3 (read as 3 to the *third power* or 3 *cubed*) yields 3 X 3 X 3 = 27, and so on. As soon as the students have a basic grasp of these mathematical ideas, they are ready to act them out.

Have the students stand, perhaps in groups of 4, behind a starting line. Note that for this first round they will "walk off" number power distances for number 2. The first participant from each group will walk forward 2^1 paces, the next individual 2^2 steps, the third person 2^3, and the fourth group member 2^4 paces; the individuals will have walked forward 2, 4, 8 and 16 steps respectively. Then ask, "How far would someone going 2^5 steps need to travel?" When the students agree on an answer, select someone to walk it off. Then what about 2^6 or 2^7?

At some point, the number of necessary steps will become too great to accomplish in a straight line and still remain on the playground. Have the students discuss and agree on an estimate of where several more powers for that number would place an individual. Next try another number, perhaps 4, and this time "hop off" the number power distances. Vary the physical activity for each new "Power Trip" and, if greater precision is desired, make use of trundle wheels, long tapes, and/or other measurement tools. All in all, your students will have gained a firm understanding of the powers of numbers—and enjoyed the experience.

Variations: (1)Try a situation where the powers remain constant, but the numbers increase in size sequentially. For example, what will result when you cube a series of numbers such as 2^3, 3^3, 4^3, 5^3 and so forth? (2) When dealing with large numbers such as 10^2, 10^3, or 50^3, 50^4, and so forth, it quickly becomes impractical to try to act out the results. In such cases, have the students estimate, and discuss where they might end up if they actually took such a "Power Trip."

NUMBER POWER ACTIONS *(Continued)*

(2⁴)

(2³)

(2²)

VII REWARD DAY ACTIVITIES

The 11 REWARD DAY ACTIVITIES in this section are designed to be used as part of a school-wide effort to recognize the positive efforts of students.

REWARD DAY OVERVIEW

The activities in this section can be used in several different ways. They can be used individually during regular physical education sessions, or they can be combined to work well as special events for individual classroom teachers. However, these Reward Day Activities are designed to be used as part of a schoolwide system to recognize the positive efforts of your students. A series of weekly, monthly, or quarterly Reward Day events can promote the enjoyment of physical activities, while motivating students to maintain good grades and citizenship in the classroom. A fun and exciting Reward Day system will help promote a positive atmosphere on any school campus.

Various approaches can be used to determine eligibility for participation in the Reward Days. All students can be allowed to participate each time and receive the benefits of the program. Some schools might choose to establish standards in areas such as academics, citizenship, playground behavior, or sportsmanship that must be met in order for an individual to participate. We feel that a fun and exciting Reward Day program will motivate students to display appropriate behavior and put forth effort in the areas deemed important at each school site.

Individual school site needs will determine how the Reward Day system is organized. One teacher might be in charge of the program and delegate responsibilities to others in order to make the program a success. The responsibility might be rotated by having one teacher in charge of one Reward Day per year. The responsibility could be shifted to the students by having the Student Council organize the Reward Days. The amount of time allowed for each Reward Day, and the number of Reward Days per year can be determined based on school needs. Many of the sets of activities are designed for sessions of approximately one hour, but activities can be combined to provide longer sessions, or some activities can be eliminated to accommodate shorter Reward Days.

Advertising and promoting the Reward Days can help make the program successful. Posters and announcements will help build enthusiasm for upcoming events. Promote the first Reward Day well, start off with a fun and exciting set of activities, and the Reward Day system will add a lot to your school!

MINI CARNIVAL

Grades: K– 6

Purposes: To provide an opportunity to improve various skills while having a great time

Equipment: Miscellaneous articles needed for the chosen events

Description: This Reward Day will work well as a schoolwide event. Each class should come up with one activity, and the result collectively will be a carnival atmosphere where everyone can have a lot of fun while practicing skills and getting lots of exercise. Examples of activities that might be set up are challenges such as tossing a ping-pong ball into a can, knocking down a stack of plastic bottles with a tennis ball, tossing a Frisbee through a hoop, blowing and catching bubbles, and so on. One teacher should supervise each event, and upper-grade students can help set up and run booths as needed.

Participants can be allowed to roam freely and choose the events they wish to try, or each person can be given a starting assignment and a rotational pattern can be established for participants to follow. A simple map posted in each classroom, indicating the events and their location on the field or in rooms will assist students during the event, as well as help build enthusiasm prior to the Reward Day. Add some authentic attire and music, and let the fun begin!

MINI CARNIVAL *(Continued)*

SPORTS SMORGASBORD

Grades: K– 6

Purposes: To provide an opportunity for all participants to engage in their favorite game or sport

Equipment: Balls, bats, cones, and whatever else is needed to play the games selected

Description: Determine the favorite sports and games of the students, and let them sample everything at the Sports Smorgasbord. Activities might include organized sports such as softball, basketball, and soccer. Other games and activities might be offered as well. The set of activities, along with the format used, will give participants the chance to play their favorite games during this Reward Day. One method is to allow players to roam the field and enter or leave the various games freely. Another approach is to blow a whistle or ring a bell every fifteen minutes or half hour, and allow players to change fields only during breaks in the action. A more structured way to organize the activity is to have people sign up for the activities beforehand, and allow only a certain number of players per field during each time period. As a way to promote enthusiasm for the upcoming event, and to help participants make good use of their time, a simple map showing the location of each activity on the field can be posted in several locations on campus.

One or more people should be assigned to supervise each game or activity. Part of the play area can be designated a "free play" area for those who do not choose to participate in an organized game, as the goal is always to have everyone thoroughly enjoy the Reward Day. For this set of activities, it might work best to have separate sessions for primary and intermediate grades. Choose several of the favorite games and activities of the group, or have them vote to decide which games to play, and get a taste of the Sports Smorgasbord.

SPORTS SMORGASBORD (Continued)

VAN GOGH WHERE YOU WANT TO

Grades: K– 6

Purposes: To encourage creativity
To promote schoolwide camaraderie
To have a ton of fun

Equipment: Whatever is necessary for the projects selected

Description: Each teacher and class should decide on a creative project that can be done with a minimal amount of materials and preparation. The teacher should stay and supervise the project, while the students participate in one or more of the projects offered elsewhere. Based on the amount of time available and the type of projects chosen, participants may be allowed to roam from room to room and complete as many projects as possible, or students might sign up ahead of time for one or two projects that interest them. If a large central area is available, such as a multipurpose room, everyone can come together to participate and watch the work of others.

A display can be set up after the event in a hallway, library, or multi-purpose room so that everyone can see examples of the finished projects. The display is a nice way to recognize the creativity of the students, and it is an excellent way to promote interest in both the activity and in the Reward Day system in general.

multi-purpose room

TALENT EXPLOSION

Grades: K– 6

Purposes: To provide an opportunity for practice in any type of physical activity
To promote schoolwide enthusiasm and excitement

Equipment: Whatever is necessary for the presentations selected

Description: Announce well in advance by distributing flyers and putting up posters that the upcoming Reward Day will feature the talents of the students. Encourage any individual, small-group, or entire-class presentations that involve physical skills. It is helpful to organize a practice session or two before the actual show in order to see how many acts there are, decide how much time each act will be allowed, and to establish the order in which they will perform. To build interest, older students can put together and post or distribute programs prior to the event.

On the day of the show, invite all the kids and their families and friends to gather in the multipurpose room or an outdoor meeting place to enjoy the presentation. To promote enthusiasm for this activity, as well as future Reward Days, take a few pictures during the show and make a display board to hang in the multipurpose room or central hallway.

OLYMPIC ADVENTURE

Grades: K–6

Purposes: To provide practice in a variety of activities
To promote school unity and cooperation

Equipment: Whatever is needed to set up the events that are chosen

Description: This event can be set up to resemble the actual Olympics as much or as little as desired. The high jump apparatus, official shot put, and so on, can be borrowed from the junior high or high school, and accurate distances can be measured and marked for races. With this format, the event can be set up as if it were an official track meet.

One alternative to the above mentioned format is to use whatever is readily available to set up various events. For example, hurdles can be made of boxes, cones, or waste baskets. A tennis ball might be substituted as the shot, a Frisbee can be thrown like a discus, and participants can use a baseball bat to pole-vault over a stack of books.

Another way to organize the event is to have each class invent a new challenge for the Fake-olympics! In this version, classes come up with rules and equipment for activities such as The 100 Yard Low Hurdles While Wearing Swim Fins, The Drag a Burlap Bag of Tennis Balls 440 Relay, and so forth. In this version, participants are sure to get plenty of exercise and a lot of laughs.

Whichever format is used, the students will get the chance to participate in some challenges and have a great time. If the activity is well-received, it can be repeated using one of the alternative formats.

Participants can be allowed to roam freely and participate in as many events as time allows, or a sign up sheet organized by grade levels and sequence of events can be posted before the event. Older students can be paired with younger ones to help them, or they can compete as pairs, with events organized accordingly. This activity is a good one for taking pictures and putting up a display board for all to enjoy after the event has taken place.

OLYMPIC ADVENTURE *(Continued)*

MELON MADNESS

Grades: K–6

Purposes: To provide an opportunity for a variety of fun activities
To provide an opportunity to incorporate academic challenges into a Reward Day
event

To enjoy a tasty treat and have lots of fun

Equipment: Watermelon, and whatever is needed for the activities selected

Description: Teachers can begin this Reward Day ahead of time by incorporating various activities into their curriculum. For example, geography and mapping skills can be taught while showing areas where watermelon is grown, or math skills involving estimation can be introduced or reinforced and used to estimate how many seeds per melon there will be.

Often a local grower or supermarket will be willing to provide enough watermelon for the activity at a reduced price. One watermelon for each class of about thirty students will work, but two per classroom will assure that all participants will get plenty to eat and be able to collect lots of seeds for the activities.

The whole school can gather together to eat the melons, or melons can be delivered to each classroom to be enjoyed. Provide each person with a small cup or plastic bag to put their seeds in for the upcoming activities. Each class should come up with an event that can be done using watermelon seeds ahead of time. Activities such as a Watermelon Seed on a Spoon Relay, Seed Pinching for Distance or Accuracy, Watermelon Seed Art, and so forth, can be interesting, entertaining, and fun! During this Reward Day, participants can learn a lot, enjoy a taste treat, and have a great time!

MELON MADNESS

GOOD OLD-FASHIONED FUN

Grades: K–6

Purposes: To provide an opportunity to participate in various challenges
To help promote a positive school atmosphere

Equipment: Whatever is needed for the activities selected

Description: It can be entertaining, informational, and a lot of fun to create a Good Old-Fashioned Fun Reward Day for present day students. Some simple equipment can be gathered and the events organized to show kids how to have fun "the old-fashioned way." The activity can be promoted ahead of time and students can be encouraged to wear old-fashioned clothes on the day of the event. To add a bit of atmosphere, teachers can round up some old-fashioned music to be played during the activities.

Stations that can be set up might include activities such as Marble Shooting, Jacks, Yo-Yo Tricks, Kite Flying, Jump Rope, and any other activities in which people at the school are interested.

Parents can be included and might have fun participating and helping the students during the event. Parents might also set up booths with cotton candy, lemonade, and hot dogs, or may take pictures of students who have dressed up in old-fashioned clothes.

Students can be allowed to roam freely and participate in as many events as time allows. Promote the activity ahead of time, create an interesting atmosphere, and have some Good Old-Fashioned Fun!

IT'S SHOW TIME

Grades: K– 6

Purposes: To provide entertainment and a learning experience
To inspire student participation in various activities

Equipment: Whatever is needed to set up for the performance

Description: If funds are available for schoolwide assemblies, many performers will bring their show to your school for a reasonable price. A myriad of interesting, informative, and entertaining presentations are offered by professionals in most every area.

Another way to provide entertainment at either a very low cost or for free is to utilize the talents possessed by members of the community. Many individuals, groups, and businesses are willing to come to schools to put on presentations of all kinds. Possible demonstrations might include performances by jugglers, jump-rope teams, bicyclists, skateboarders, rollerbladers, karate teachers, yo-yo experts, gymnasts, and whatever else the students might find interesting.

Often these demonstrations will inspire the students to practice and participate in similar activities after seeing the presentation. Promoting the show ahead of time, and providing opportunities for involvement afterwards, will make this Reward Day fun and educational.

bicycling

skateboarding

martial arts

gymnastics

skaters

OBSTACLES EVERYWHERE

Grades: K–6

Purposes: To provide an unlimited number of physical challenges
To give participants a chance to create their own activities

Equipment: Whatever is needed for the courses designed

Description: Each class can be responsible for creating an obstacle course for the others to enjoy. On the day of this event, the teacher can supervise the course, while members of the class experience as many of the other courses as possible. People can be allowed to roam freely, or a pattern can be established for everyone to follow so that all participants get a chance to try each course.

Simple equipment can be used in an infinite number of ways to create obstacle courses that are challenging and fun. Old bike tires, buckets, boxes, cones, balls, balloons, rope, boards, and countless other materials that can be found at school or home can be arranged in a myriad of ways resulting in entertaining, demanding, and innovative obstacle courses. Courses can be set up to have pairs competing against each other, with individuals trying to record the fastest time, or groups working together in relay fashion to complete the course.

Most everyone enjoys the challenge of an obstacle course. This activity also provides students with an opportunity to help create activities for others. Classes can add art, music, and whatever else they can think of to enhance their courses. Don't let anything stand in your way as you prepare for and participate in Obstacles Everywhere Reward Day!

PARENTS/TEACHERS/STUDENTS REWARD DAY

Grades: K–6

Purposes: To promote unity and good parent/teacher/student relations
                To get exercise and have fun together

Equipment: Whatever is needed for the activities chosen

Description: Getting everyone involved in the school to play together can be fun and help build cohesiveness and rapport between parents, teachers, and students. Any combination of these groups playing on the same team, or against each other can provide a great time, some healthy exercise, and help increase the camaraderie at school.

Activities can range from softball to soccer or basketball, to having parents and teachers participate in any of the Reward Day activities presented in this book, or in Reward Day events that are developed at your school. Promote the activity to build interest and enthusiasm, and get everyone together for some fun and fitness!

THE LAST BLAST

Grades: K– 6

Purposes: To provide an opportunity to participate in various challenges
To get together and have a blast one last time

Equipment: Whatever is needed for the activities chosen

Description: The Last Blast can be used as the final Reward Day of the school year. Create a set of exceptionally thrilling events as a way to celebrate the good behavior of the students throughout the year.

Many exciting and innovative activities can be set up without spending a lot of money. A log or length of large plastic pipe can be suspended horizontally with mats placed underneath and two people can play Pillow Pow on a Pole. A long sheet of plastic can be used as a Slip-n-slide. Water balloons can be thrown at a target. An area can be designated for Sprinkler Sports (play tag, soccer or tug-of-war, while in range of the sprinklers). Special equipment such as a Dunk Tank, Earthball, or Parachute can be borrowed or rented. Participants can be allowed to roam freely and experience as many activities as possible.

Parent volunteers and P.T.A. members should be encouraged to help with the event. Volunteers might set up booths for Face Painting, Bubble Creations, and Food and Drinks. Parents can also help supervise or participate in the events.

Create a special Reward Day extravaganza to honor the students for whatever criteria is appropriate for your school, and have one Last Blast!

THE LAST BLAST (Continued)

APPENDIX

— *Equipment* —

EQUIPMENT LIST

Balloons

Bases

Basketballs

Beanbags

Bicycle Tires

Blankets

Boxes

Buckets

Cones

Earthball

Foam Balls

Footbags

Football Flags

Footballs

Hoops

Juggling Balls

Kickballs

Paper Plates

Parachute

Plastic Bottles and Jugs

Playground Balls

Rope

Scarves

Sheets

Soccer Balls

Softball Bats

Softballs

String

T-ball Stand

Tennis Balls

Tennis Racket

Video Camera

Volleyball Net

Volleyballs

Yarn

SUGGESTIONS FOR
OBTAINING EQUIPMENT

Hopefully, most or all of the equipment needed to implement the activities presented in this book can be found at your school site. If not, in most cases, the items needed can be made by, or gathered from parents and community members. A sample request letter is included on the following page for your convenience.

EQUIPMENT REQUEST LETTER

Dear _____:

Our class is collecting a set of homemade Physical Education equipment. We can use materials that may be in your home, or at your work site, that are no longer being used. Our goal is to have enough equipment to allow all students the opportunity for maximum participation in each activity. You can help us accomplish our goal by donating any of the following items:

1. _____

2. _____

3. _____

4. _____

5. _____

We appreciate your help! These materials will provide a great deal of exercise and enjoyment during the school year.

Sincerely,